The
Southern Way

The regular volume for the Southern devotee

Kevin Robertson

Issue 49

www.crecy.co.uk

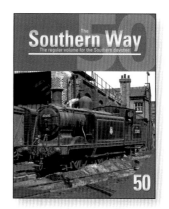

ISBN 9781909328938

First published in 2020 by Noodle Books
an imprint of Crécy Publishing Ltd

New contact details
All editorial submissions to:
The Southern Way (Kevin Robertson)
'Silmaril'
Upper Lambourn
Hungerford
Berkshire RG17 8QR
Tel: 01488 674143
editorial@thesouthernway.co.uk

A CIP record for this book is available from the
British Library

Publisher's note: Every effort has been made to
identify and correctly attribute photographic
credits. Any error that may have occurred is
entirely unintentional.

Printed in the UK by Cambrian Printers Ltd

Noodle Books is an imprint of
Crécy Publishing Limited
1a Ringway Trading Estate
Shadowmoss Road
Manchester M22 5LH

www.crecy.co.uk

Issue No 50 of THE SOUTHERN WAY
ISBN 9781909328952
available in April 2020 at £14.95

To receive your copy the moment it is
released, order in advance from your usual
supplier, or it can be sent post-free (UK)
direct from the publisher:

Crécy Publishing Ltd (Noodle Books)

1a Ringway Trading Estate, Shadowmoss
Road, Manchester M22 5LH

Tel 0161 499 0024

www.crecy.co.uk

enquiries@crecy.co.uk

Front cover:
A trio of 2Bil sets 'somewhere' on the 'Portsmouth Direct'.
The code '57' indicates a Waterloo-Portsmouth/Southsea
stopping service via Worplesdon. Of particular note has to
be the pronounced periscope. *P. W. Gray/GWP*

Rear cover:
Pegasus running as 'The Trianon Bar' in the formation of
the 'Golden Arrow', seen at Dover Marine in June 1963.
Graham Smith

Title page:
Yes, you can (just) see semaphore signals on the
Southern. This is Marchwood with the up starting signals
which now spend nearly all their time in the 'on'
position. The two arms explain that the loop here is
signalled for bi-directional working. Marchwood is the
fringe of the MAS area controlled from Basingstoke.
What price also common sense? A perfectly good railway
lies moribund whilst our supposed 'representatives'
prevaricate over the difference it would make to traffic
congestion in the area or hide behind the 'not enough
pathways/stock available' banner. Perhaps they should
travel (attempt would be more like) on the A35/A326 at
peak times. No one is asking for a 15-minute regular
interval working, but peak hour trains cannot fail to
make a difference. But then did we or our forefathers not
say exactly the same 30-40+ years ago when closures
were all the rage (not just in Hampshire of course). And
we were not listened to then... *Mike King*

Contents

Introduction

The trouble with producing a quarterly journal is that something which is topical when I sit down at the computer is invariably 'old-hat' by the time the next issue appears on the shelves. Be assured this is not a suggestion or idea that I or the publishers have to increase or change the frequency of 'SW' but a statement of fact about which I can do nothing.

Consequently, by the time you read this it will be at least three months after it was written so it is possible that the news which follows may already be known to some. That news is that at least two more businesses have started up producing railway books. This is not an issue to me especially if it adds to our knowledge but what does worry a little is one (I will be respectful and will not mention a name) story I have heard where the person in charge of one of these concerns thought it a good idea if the cover of their first book depicted a locomotive – I think it was LMS – in a livery never carried.

As I said, I am all for more information becoming available, but please do not manipulate things for the sake of fashion, sales or marketing. I would follow this up by saying, if you notice a book – regardless of publisher – with errors, and here I include SW, do let the publisher know. I have oft said, the perfect book has never been written nor produced and we need to try to be as accurate as possible.

Changing subject completely, I come on to what was to have been the lead article in this issue of SW, 'The oil burning engines of the SR'. I say 'was' as 8,000 words and 80 images later (some duplicates amongst these) I thought we had covered all there was reasonable to find. But that was until I was given the lead to ... well, shall we say a new source that may yield surprising results, so please bear with me and all will, I promise, be revealed as soon as possible.

Instead, we have brought forward what was to have been the lead in our celebratory Issue No 50, which is the start of the story of John Click. If you have never heard of him I will be slightly surprised but I promise it is worth reading and I sincerely hope you will enjoy this first instalment.

I have of course already broken a convention with this Editorial in referring to a feature within the actual issue, my choice being normally to allow each article to speak for itself. But I am now going to do it a second time and comment slightly on our book review of Gilbert *Szlumper and Leo Amery of the Southern Railway*, respectively General Manager and Director of the SR – see page 96 of this issue. I will admit to having been aware of this book before and I will also have to admit my initial preconceived notions have been completely shattered.

It is my habit, if a new work comes out on a favourite topic, be that a locomotive type, route or specific ancillary topic, to actively seek it out and hopefully add a little more to my store of information. I would hardly expect that to be the case with a book of the type so described but I will freely admit I was wrong and I think have gained more from this work than I could ever have imagined.

Speaking once more of books, I will not, out of respect, mention the author or publisher for the present, but do look out for a new work on signalling, hopefully due soon. Excellent author, similar publisher and one I look forward to adding to my shelves in the near future.

Enough, though, of the plugs and, as I have said before with SW, 'forward once more to the past' and this time with just one last thought. April 2020 will see our 50th issue: a definite milestone and one which I know I have said before I honestly never thought we would reach. For those of you who have come this far, a sincere thank you, but please don't stop at 49: do make it a round number at least!

Kevin Robertson

Attracting the attention of the second man in the 'Western' in the departure platform, No 34094 *Mortehoe* breaks new ground as it arrives at Birmingham Snow Hill on 27 April 1963. Southampton Football Club had reached the semi-final of the FA Cup for 1962/63 with a match against Manchester United to be played at Villa Park. Several excursions from the coast were run that day for the benefit of fans, all of which helped the crowd who attended the game to reach 65,000. Whilst no doubt in high spirits on the way to Birmingham, it was a subdued journey home as Southampton lost 1-0. One month later Manchester United would be the victors in the final against Leicester City at Wembley. *Corbis images*

John Gayward Click
'Engineering the Southern' Part 1

The name John Click will likely be familiar to most readers of *SW*, at least the ones who follow steam and have a penchant for the work of Mr Bulleid.

What, more on Mr Bulleid? I can hear the cry now, 'and what more is there left to say?' At this point it is all too easy for a writer (in this case the Editor) to attempt to justify their production with the oft overdone superlative, 'new information' etc. etc. in reality little than a marketing ploy intended to entice a potential audience to part with their hard-earned cash. But this series is, I promise, genuinely different; indeed, when I first read the Click notes I was addicted, not just because they contain new information but because they also answered many of the questions I (and I am sure others) have long wondered about Mr Bulleid and the influence both he and his designs had upon the contemporary railway scene.

The Click text, of necessity, deserves an introduction devoted just to itself. As referred to above, the target audience has to be those who have already digested most if not all of what has been previously transcribed to paper on Mr Bulleid and his work. By that I mean the RCTS volumes, *The Book of the Merchant Navy Pacifics* and *The Book of the West Country and Battle of Britain Pacifics* by Irwell Press, the biographies on

Mr Bulleid by Sean Day Lewis and H. A. V. Bulleid, John Fry's excellent work on the 'Merchant Navy' class and my own efforts on 'Leader' and *Bulleid – Man, Myth and Machines*. To have a working knowledge of all the above will be a good starting point for what follows – and again I promise there will be many new revelations in the next few issues. (I do appreciate more recent books on the work of Mr Bulleid published by Pen & Sword have appeared and which I am sure are equally useful but these I have yet to personally study in detail.)

The reader could also be excused for wondering what might there be left to say on the same topic? Up to very recently I would have agreed. I base that assumption on my own studies: odd snippets, for example, have emerged on No 36001 plus the

John G. Click (right) together with unknown prior to a trip on the footplate of the 'Golden Arrow'. A steam man through and through, 'JGC' was a capable engineer who aligned himself with Bulleid and in a railway career of 20+ years also gained experience on all the latter's steam designs – we cannot be certain if he had practical experience on the Co-Co electrics or the main line diesels. Seen in the background, No 35028 appears in pristine (original) condition and is likely recorded at Stewart's Lane. With little if any dirt visible anywhere, the clasp brakes, one of Bulleid's definite successes, show up well. Possibly the only negative aspect is the sandbox fillers, which have not been slid across to the closed position.

occasional illustration but nothing of real substance. I suspect for those far more expert than I on the topic of the Pacifics, the same would apply. Straight away I would also comment that that is not in any way meant to imply we know all there is to know. Research into any historical area, be that mankind, warfare, monarchy or even railways, will often result in new information throwing up questions which had not previously been considered; in other words, we may know the bones but the flesh has melted away.

Similarly, there will also be rumour and suggestion but this of course needs to be substantiated from respected sources, or if used at least referenced as being a proposition. The facts are already known: it is how so many of the facts came to be that we are now able to explain.

It is with the last statement in mind that I will now introduce John Click, a professionally trained engineer who worked with Bulleid in various roles and had much experience in working with many of Bulleid's creations.

In the course of my own research into No 36001 I had not only heard of but also later met John Click. There was also a persistent rumour he had prepared his own story of Mr Bulleid; I for one longed to read it, certain it would yield new information – when that time eventually came my assessment was right.

But this manuscript was hard to find. Again there were rumours it had been commissioned, written, rejected, serialised in various railway magazines, and such like. There was even talk that with the passing of John Click it had been destroyed. Despite enquiries to various publishers there was never any definite confirmation. That is, until 2016 when, on a hunch, a trawl through 'Search Engine' at the National Railway Museum (NRM) revealed a clue. Suffice to say I was on my way to York almost on the next available train!

What I found was a *partial* draft: text supplemented by handwritten notes – not always easy to transcribe and regrettably as well with pieces missing. The other problem was that it consisted of a series of pages not in any specific order. There are clear gaps and also much duplication – perhaps the same page drafted two or even three times with odd sentences added or removed. The result is that topics are carried over/brought back/forward/not completed … in all, certainly not easy to follow, and as I mentioned, not in any way in order of date or subject. Continuity, then, is a definite problem.

Even so it was too good to ignore so the next question was how best to proceed, and after much deliberation the results are before you now. Unfortunately, politics now also come into play and the result is a serialisation rather than a new book; certainly, after much thought, I do genuinely believe this is probably also the best way to present his notes. With none of the main players in the story of Mr Bulleid still with us, including John Click himself, this must likely be the last 'new' word on the subject.

Of necessity as well, this must also be a rather longer introduction/explanation to a series than we have needed previously and consequently the best place to commence has to be an introduction to John Click himself.

John Gayward Click (JGC) joined the Southern Railway in 1943 as a premium apprentice aged 17. As he states later, he was probably one of the very few individuals who had experience with all the locomotives and rolling stock designed by Bulleid (OVB), including the 'Turf Burner', being thus able to effect comparisons with other machines operating at the same time.

His recollections comprise both the objective and the subjective. It is quickly apparent he was an ardent steam man, and also, as time passed, it becomes clear he falls under the spell of Bulleid – for better or worse.

Such reverence for one's guru is not, of course, unusual. A respected teacher, lecturer, professor or employer can have a profound influence on a young brain, sometimes as in the case of JGC for the rest of his life. Admiration is one thing but it later becomes clear with JGC this turns into almost reverence, a behaviour which can also risk bringing about a blinkered approach. The 'pupil' is then unable to recognise the good from the bad, and so whilst JGC at times does indeed pass constructive comment, on other occasions he either glosses over or even seems to ignore completely what to even non-technical readers is the blindingly obvious.

At this stage we must also say JGC was without doubt a gifted and skilled engineer but also one who at times believed himself better than others and who could be both dismissive and also ruthless if anyone dared challenge his personal views. (I was to experience this particular side of his character myself.)

At the time JGC joined the Southern Railway the country was still in the grip of war. Bulleid was also approaching the peak of his power and influence; this would come in the few short years between the restoration of peace in the summer of 1945 and nationalisation in 1948. Being in his privileged position, albeit in a very junior capacity, JGC had some contact with and also came to know the senior men charged with implementing the ideas of 'The Chief'. Of course, as time passed, so JGC became more and more involved and although it is not specifically mentioned we may take it that it was during this time that he also came to the notice of Bulleid.

The reason for this is explained by nationalisation. Headquarters at Marylebone were quick to identify that company loyalties would, unless addressed, lead to an entrenchment of ideas, hence the transfer of senior men from Brighton to other workshops and later the movement of R. G. Jarvis in the other direction. As we also know, Bulleid retired from BR in September 1949 and subsequently moved to take charge of CIE in Ireland in 1949/50. (The reader is referred to *A Lifetime with Locomotives* by R. C. Bond, Goose & Sons, 1975, for further detail on the attempt to amalgamate the CME's departments of the four companies into BR.)

In the early 1950s and with a non-Southern man now in charge at Brighton, the Bulleid influence was immediately less pronounced. Whereas in the past Bulleid expected and indeed had the support of all his senior staff with all he did, now that he was absent any criticism of his designs was no longer the 'taboo' subject it may once have been. The new Chief was Robin Riddles, based at Marylebone, and senior staff recognised that for the sake of their own careers loyalties needed to be transferred. I have heard it said before, although I cannot recall where, that whilst Bulleid was certainly regarded as a 'breath of fresh air' when he arrived in 1938, by the late 1940s with his ideas becoming seemingly ever more revolutionary, there were those who now wished to distance themselves from such diktats, akin as I was told to a chief leading his sheep to the edge of cliff. Nationalisation thus gave some the opportunity to escape.

Accordingly, to find the support he needed in Ireland, Bulleid would now have to look below the previous senior level to lower tiers and it is thus that JGC comes to notice. For JGC the timing was also perfect. In order to maintain continuity so far as BR were now concerned JGC was also the ideal man, having had some experience with No 2039 and also with the trials of 'Leader'.

As to why it was Click (plus one other) who were later seconded to Bulleid in Ireland we can only surmise and it would be wrong to speculate. The obvious answer was that it was in order for the two men involved to gain engineering experience. There is no specific evidence to suggest Click was asked for personally, but he had been involved in the trials of No 36001, a fact likely known to Bulleid, so for this reason alone he may have been requested. It really matters not how it came about. We might well imagine the BRB being relieved when Bulleid announced his intention to retire; possibly the offer/acceptance of staff to assist later in Ireland – if required – may even have sealed the deal.

What is very apparent is that JGC, like Bulleid, was an ardent 'steam man'. Arguably this might also have been his downfall later. Certainly he was ambitious, indeed his private notes comment that his youthful ambition was to achieve the status of Chief Mechanical Engineer of the Southern. Again surmising, but coming forward to the 1960s, steam was definitely seen as yesterday's traction: anyone with an interest in steam was similarly yesterday's man. JGC may well have been viewed as too entrenched to change yet too young to retire. We can imagine him becoming disillusioned, angry perhaps at what he witnessed happening around him, hence his departure from the railway industry and a new career in education, for without doubt he was undoubtedly a highly talented individual.

If JGC had one fault, and it is with caution that this is expressed (if for no other reason than we are all afflicted with failings of one sort or another), then it was his apparent inability to communicate with others and equally his inability to listen at times. Those who met him could easily be put off by a brusque and sharp manner; one might even describe him as cutting. Clearly that did not apply to all he communicated with but it appears there was a distinct 'them and us' attitude: something about the professional classes, which he certainly considered he was in, being better than the rest. Any attempt

Urie 'Arthur' No 755 *The Red Knight* in clean wartime livery with Bulleid lettering and, more important, Bulleid modifications to the front end with a large-diameter chimney. John Click would see members of the class working (as he puts it) in fine fettle and maintained in clean condition, even if plainly overloaded at times.

by a perceived 'lower level' individual making contact was to be dismissed as if swatting an unwanted speck. As an example of this behaviour, later in his role of Assistant Works Manager at Eastleigh he was prone to fits of temper, casting doubts on the skills and knowledge of senior foremen at the works, such as Harry Frith, and on one occasion he is also reported as throwing a chair across a meeting room. What drove him to such outbursts, again we may only speculate about, for he could also be most gracious at other times – but on the occasions known of by the author such congenial conduct appears to have been mainly when he was involved with one of equal, or what he considered to be 'senior', rank or intellect.

As if to make up for what seemingly became 'a chip on his shoulder' at having seen the life of his beloved steam engines foreshortened and his own anticipated railway career curtailed, he made direct contact with Bulleid himself. (Perhaps, even, this was how he came to the attention of OVB.) The JGC files contain numerous letters sent to OVB, as well as references to occasional meetings with him, but I suspect JGC believed himself to be closer to Bulleid than he actually was, not least as JGC admits he regrets he never once met Mrs Bulleid.

But have no doubt, JGC was certainly liked (probably the wrong verb) by Anthony Bulleid (OVS's son) as well. Following the

death of O. V. S. Bulleid, the Click files at the NRM contain much correspondence between JGC and Anthony and he was clearly a major contributor to Anthony's own book *Bulleid of the Southern*. Anthony Bulleid was also a mechanical engineer by profession but his own career path took him away from the railway industry, although this was where he had originally trained.

We may suspect that the publication of the 'son's excellent book on the father' (Ian Allan, 1977) may well have delayed publication of any manuscript JGC was contemplating at that time. From surviving correspondence at the NRM I also get the impression that my own first book on 'Leader' (Alan Sutton, 1988), may have similarly contributed to a further delay. Let me say straight away that was never my intention but there was certainly some rather cutting correspondence between JGC and HAV (Anthony Bulleid was in fact Henry Anthony Vaughan Bulleid) around this time, and not concerning any dispute between the two men!

As has been referred to earlier, the JGC archive at the NRM also contains much original correspondence from JGC to OVS Bulleid, between JGC and Anthony Bulleid and from other individuals to Bulleid senior. The fact this was in the JGC papers we may take as a clear indication that the Bulleid family both trusted and respected JGC and was happy for him to hold part of the family archive.

The unmistakable outline of No 36001, the only 'Leader ever to take to the rails under steam. As well as witnessing the hilarious attempts when the engine first moved under steam – *to be recounted in a future instalment of these memoirs, Ed* – JGC was also present on the engine during a number of the trials.

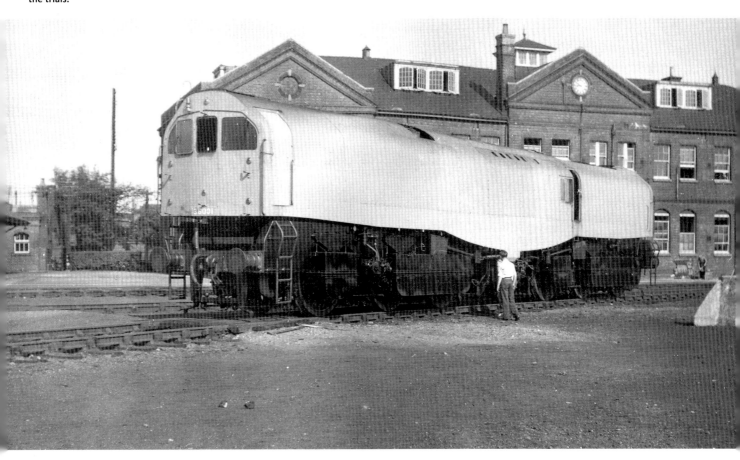

Other than a few articles by JGC in *Steam World/Steam Railway* many years ago, little actually attributable to JGC has appeared in print. We know his interest in steam remained for the rest of his life as he took a great interest in the work of the few who were still attempting to promote the cause of steam, notably Livio Dante Porta in Argentina and David Wardale in South Africa. For a time, also, he was 'on the circuit' giving talks. I recall attending one (but kept a deliberately low profile) advertised as 'Working with Bulleid'. I certainly looked forward to a fascinating evening. Unfortunately, it instead consisted of what appeared to be a series of holiday slides of his trips to South America with little if any mention of steam. At times, as well, throughout the evening JGC appeared confused and seemingly oblivious to the fidgeting of his audience.

Regardless of his abilities or otherwise as a speaker, or any health issues there may have been, his technical know-how was renowned at several of the preservation societies and he deservedly received senior status.

From my own limited dealings with him I would surmise that he was an extremely talented individual, perhaps even in the same mould as O. V. S. Bulleid himself – although I never had the privilege of meeting the great man. JGC was, though, seemingly incapable of considering (or at the very least unwilling to consider) any point of view other than his own – not a fault in itself but one which may well have contributed to his own restricted railway career. Even so we may justifiably regard his legacy as providing probably the clearest indication we will ever have of what it was like to be 'Engineering the Southern'.

The early years

JGC commences his memoirs at the age of five, circa 1931, when the family (his father was a teacher) moved into a house at Lee backing on to what was then referred to as the Dartford Loop Line. Aside from the ability to observe trains, his interest in engineering may well have originated in some pre-owned Meccano passed on from a family whose own offspring had grown away from it. In later correspondence with OVB it appears that he too shared a similar interest in the same toy. Two years later Click was a regular reader of the *Meccano Magazine*, devouring especially the railway information therein and which seemed to a young impressionable mind to feature LNER Pacifics in profusion compared with the 0-6-0 and 4-4-0 types to be seen locally.

An acquaintance made on holiday in 1936 resulted in a visit to new friends, who lived in what is today Haringey and from where he was to see 'in the flesh' his first 'A3', 'V2' and, towards the end of the day, an 'A4'. Unfortunately, it was not to be the euphoric climax as might be otherwise expected for *Quicksilver* was in poor external condition, '… dirty silver was not a patch on clean apple green'.

We have no confirmed month/day for his birth (he died in 1988) but we do know that the year after his LNER experience he was taken by his mother to County Hall where arrangements were made for his next school.

Officialdom satisfied, the next visit that day was to Waterloo

where he found his way to the end of Platform 11 through the simple expedient then possible of dodging over the buffers of the engine dock – a trick used by generations of spotters. A 'King Arthur', No 780, was standing at the concourse end of Platform 11 unable to get out and back to Nine Elms as another engine opposite the signal box had derailed – none other than *Lord Howe* sporting its enlarged, and to a young boy 'magnificent', new boiler. He watched as vans were quickly brought up from the depot by an ancient (undescribed) 0-4-4T and men quickly got to work around the tender, which had likely split the points.

This was just one of many subsequent visits to Waterloo, no doubt encouraged by his earlier experience. King's Cross quickly became another favourite but on each occasion he failed to see a blue 'A4' as hoped. By early 1938 he was going up to King's Cross on his own most Saturdays, by which time there was always a chance of seeing a new 'A4' on each occasion. He would wait for the 'Flying Scotsman' to come in on Platform 1 and then get the No 77 bus back to Charing Cross. On one of these visits an 'A4', No 4468, named *Mallard,* arrived, and for whatever reason he recalled thinking, 'Crikey … that's a duck'! (A very fast duck as it turned out!) The driver looked friendly and in consequence he was soon on the footplate. Something extraordinary then happened, for, as he describes, '… imperceptibly at first, King's Cross began to slide: we were moving! I had ridden the length of King's Cross on her. That was a good start.'

Moving ahead in years (briefly) he would often wonder if he ever saw, even met, Sir Nigel Gresley, who also waited to see the 'Scotsman', in particular the summer non-stop.

Whenever lack of funds dictated, observations were made nearer to home. He would go to Bromley South where there was a good vantage point from the footbridge over the platform. He was also astute enough to notice change was in the air as one by one 'Lord Nelsons' began appearing with different chimneys, described as '… stark, large diameter ones from which the exhaust flopped quietly instead of roaring vertically. A knowledgeable boy from Whitgift, whose school produced their own railway magazine, said the altered "Nelsons" were very much improved and it was soon clear they were working the most important expresses.' Mr Bulleid was at work, although at the time the name was not known to either JGC or the boy from Whitgift.

JGC recounts his favourite engine of the time was No 857 *Lord Howe*, then based at Stewarts Lane and frequently chosen to work the 2.00pm 'Boat' from Victoria. At the time No 857 had not been so modified and in consequence, he recalls, seemed to make a huge noise going about her work. Soon afterwards he got up early specially to see the up 'Night Ferry' and was horrified to find it hauled by two 4-4-0s instead of *Lord Howe*. Further signs of change came when 'Schools' class engines started to appear through Hither Green with new chimneys, first No 914, then a different version on No 937. There was also change at Waterloo where a number of 'Schools' appeared in a new, rather brash, bright malachite green to work the 'Bournemouth Limited'.

This was by now 1939 and JGC refers to rumours of war.

The apparent technical superiority of Germany was also brought home to him at Croydon where every afternoon an FW200 Condor of Lufthansa climbed away from the airfield displaying the swastika. To a young mind it appeared all too modern and compared favourably with the ancient biplane bombers occasionally seen on air exercises in Kent.

Two days before war started JGC was evacuated by train to Ashford and thence by bus on to Wye from where he made his first acquaintance with Ashford Works, through gaps in the sleeper fence in the Newtown Road. He would of course later get to know Ashford very well. In June the following year he returned to London in the thick of Operation 'Dynamo' and the associated railway operation that managed to move all those thousands of men to billets around the country; he recalls it as being unforgettable. Because of the fear of aerial bombardment he was soon on the move again, this time to Gillingham in Dorset, for 'onwards distribution' to Buckhorn Weston and a billet alongside the main West of England line. Here he was able to observe 'King Arthurs', particularly those from Exmouth Junction, in fine fettle, clean and reliable, though plainly overloaded at times.

Locally John's interest in railways quickly became known and in February 1941 the village shopkeeper sent him a small newspaper cutting with the most exciting railway news he had received. The Southern now had a Pacific, the name of Mr

Bulleid was also mentioned and JGC was quick to start putting things together. 'He must be the one who was altering the "Nelsons", "Schools" and now No 792 *Sir Hervis*, the latter in the new colour scheme and sporting a more shapely large-diameter chimney.'

There was what seemed an interminable wait to find out more until the April *Meccano Magazine* appeared but eventually there it was, a 'Merchant Navy' on the front cover *(see accompanying caption note)*.

But John had yet to see the engine 'in the flesh' so to speak (or should that really be 'in the metal'?). That is, until August when a message came, this time from a ganger in the village, that she was coming down next day. Concerned in case he might be perceived as a spy, JGC built a 'hide' *(he does not elaborate on this)* and waited. Soon there was a sound – a whistle – meaning the engine had left the tunnel and then going much slower than expected she drifted down – on a goods train. A definite let down. Even so, from her appearance she was decked out to impress, a fast-looking express engine certainly, and even more gaudy than appeared on the magazine cover, but she did slip by, hardly making a sound. Just a quiet noise from the rods contrasting with the 'ting – ting – tang – tong – ting – ting' etc from the wagons, one with its handbrake lever left down in the self-destruct mode, and at the end the squealing brake-van.

Gresley 'A4' No 4499 *Pochard* (*Sir Murrough Wilson* from April 1939) stands at King's Cross together with an unidentified member of the same class behind. The silver livery may have looked fine when new and in publicity shots but, as pointed out by John Click and indeed seen here, it weathered badly. Even so, one cannot fail to be impressed by the 'A4' design – the front end of which is said to owe more than a little to the hand of Mr Bulleid! *P. Kirkbright/collection KJR*

Evacuation from London. We do not pretend for one moment this relates to JGC himself but is merely an example of the period.

VOL. XXVI. N°.6. JUNE 1941

MECCANO
MAGAZINE

SOUTHERN

21C 1

S.R. "CHANNEL PACKET"
(See page 183.)

6^d

The June 1941 cover of the *Meccano Magazine*. JGC has it as the April issue but I think we can forgive a slight slip of the memory. ('April' depicted a seaplane tender.)

Writing his memoirs some decades later, he understandably knew nothing at the time of the politics that had almost led to Bulleid's first 10 'mixed-traffic' locomotives being set aside, unfinished, in favour of more urgent war work. In his own words again: '"Mixed traffic" that's a good one ...' whilst he also admits they were not very reliable. One by one he observed all 10 and always, it seemed, on the same goods working. We now of course know the reason for this as well: Missenden had banished all 10 from working into Waterloo for fear of failure and the congestion that could quickly ensue *(interesting point: when a locomotive ceases to work as it should, it is a 'failure'; never, it seems, a 'breakdown')* and instead they were to be found on goods services primarily west of Salisbury. The famed Bulleid Christmas card from 1941 showing one of the type working freight and intended to justify their 'mixed traffic' status was in effect nearer the truth than might be imagined.

Luck also had it that one morning No 21C3 was observed limping back to Eastleigh light engine and was held at Gillingham whilst the freight it was following slogged on up to Semley. With the appropriate words to the driver JGC was quickly up in the cab where the first observation was the heat, but he was shown the lot and admits the crew would probably have taken him on to Semley if he had asked.

No 21C2 *Union Castle* at Exmouth Junction with clear evidence of a casing fire. JGC was quick to point out weaknesses elsewhere but he makes little mention of the shortcomings of the Bulleid designs. At this stage, too, some comments by Gilbert Szlumper (taken from John King's book on Szlumpler and Avery reviewed later in this issue) may not go amiss. Szlumper, when invited to visit Eastleigh Works in 1941 to view the first of the class, was less than complimentary about the external design. He writes in his diary, 'This loco is distinctly ugly, too bluff fore and aft to have the appearance of streamlining. I said it looked like a cabin trunk …' Later on he was a bit more complimentary when referring to the cab and '… grand tractive effort', but he returns to his original theme with, 'I think it is a fine loco but a pity they did not shape it to fall easier on the eye.' On that basis, we may wonder what Szlumper ever thought of the 'Q'!

The same engine was seen again soon after – suitably repaired – this time on passenger stock, usually trains of 16 vehicles, which it simply played with, hurling the lot over Semley Summit *(1 in 145 heading west and the steeper 1 in 100 coming east)* either way at speeds quite unknown to anything previously. Reliability, it was said, was still a problem but days at Gillingham Grammar School were now more enjoyable as they were punctuated not just by the wretched lesson bell but also by the joyful whistling as the 'Packets' got into their true element.

As he recalls, the last green one of these was No 21C4 *(before the rest emerged in all over black)*, the green colour perhaps catching the eye of an enemy pilot who managed to shoot it up at Whimple. It seems too the wartime 60mph may not have been always complied with 100+ miles west of Waterloo, for in referring to the incident he adds, '… at least it presented a fast moving target. I always felt that the advent of the "Merchant Navies" to Exeter put paid to the official wartime 60mph order as far as that line was concerned.'

Railways were not JGC's only interest at the time as he lived not far from the aircraft manufacturer Westland at Yeovil and on fine days would often see a twin-engine fighter following the course of the main line. This was the Westland Whirlwind, a 360mph fighter-bomber which was hampered by its short operational range compared with other contemporary aircraft. With a growing interest in flight he joined the Air Training Corps at Gillingham. Notwithstanding the all-pervading security in place in 1942, the Corps was sent to Boscombe Down, at the time a top-secret establishment high on Salisbury Plain where every type of aircraft was evaluated and sometimes found wanting. The whole Corps also went up in one prototype or another. JGC comments he was not very lucky as his trip was in a Wellington powered by Pratt & Witney twin Wasp engines. Immediately after take-off they found the sky full of aircraft of every kind, from Hectors hauling Hotspur gliders to pre-production Stirlings, all doing their own thing. As a result the pilot asked where he would like to go but also wanted a bearing to get there and an ETA; JGC had a quick thought that the wartime 'Atlantic Coast Express' could not be far away and so gave the pilot a course for Red Post Junction just outside Andover, hoping no doubt to find a 'Merchant Navy' in charge. The aircraft was only at about 3,000 feet when sure enough dead ahead was some exhaust lying flat along a train. 'There it is lad,' the pilot exclaimed – for a brief moment there was a fear it might be a goods but it was indeed the 'ACE', although on this occasion in charge of a very clean malachite green 'Lord Nelson'.

The shot up No 21C4 at Exmouth Junction. The image was first used by us in *SW Special No 5. 'Wartime Southern Part 2'* and is worth repeating in part. *'On 18 November 1942, when little more than a year old, "Merchant Navy" No 21C4* Cunard White Star *was heading a goods train near Whimple when it was attacked by a low flying enemy bomber. Whilst some shells did hit the locomotive, it was two covered vans immediately next to the tender that took the full blast and immediately burst into flames. The train was stopped, parted, and the engine crew together with the guard attempted to fight the blaze as best as possible until assistance arrived. No. 21C4 was photographed a few days later at Exmouth Junction with much of its casing removed, no doubt to check for damage, before being taken away for repairs.'* As an aside, again from the Special No 5, *'... What was less known was the contents of the vehicles that caught fire; bacon and ham. The fact that both foods were by now severely rationed would have done little to cool the tempers of the men involved, subjected to such aroma and yet unable to partake. After repair, the loco subsequently returned to its then home shed of Exmouth Junction.'* This was of course not the only time rural Somerset was the target of the enemy as Castle Cary was bombed on September 1942 and unfortunately with worse results. *Jeremy Cobb collection*

(He encountered some unusual aircraft in his experience – the Wellington with P&W Wasps was a rarity, and the Hawker Hector was a pre-war biplane, single-engined, for army co-operation, and its use as a glider tug was for training only.)

It appears his ATC experiences had also instilled a love of aircraft so when the time came for a career choice, aviation – engineering or flight is not specified –was the undoubted first choice. Unfortunately, an unspecified breathing ailment meant he was quickly declared unsuitable to be a flier. This meant he was also asked to leave the ATC, which he admits was a dreadful time.

A second choice was to try for a cadetship in the REME, a decision that came about in consequence of some input from the chemistry master at Shaftesbury Grammar School which was where he spent his last year of schooling. Again, though, it was to be disappointment for despite having passed the selection board at Andover Town Hall, he failed the same day, again on the medical.

Totally devastated there were (literal) black thoughts about the prospect of being drafted down a coal mine, a prospect he dreaded greatly. Railways then began to figure in his thoughts and accordingly his father wrote to Waterloo to enquire about a premium apprenticeship/pupilage.

'Can see you here tomorrow three o'clock. Bulleid. SR. Waterloo' said the curt telegram. Father and son travelled together, changing trains at Salisbury, from where No 21C8

Waterloo concourse September 1940 – the nearest we can get to a view (without the bombs) of JGC's interview with Bulleid in the offices in 1943. The main offices are of course behind the camera. *Spence collection*

Orient Line was on the front, '… painted black, very dirty and with some holes kicked in the casing to get at various pipes underneath.' We do not know if this was his first trip east to Waterloo, possibly it was, the journey notable only for the sprint through Basingstoke which to an impressionable young mind appeared unwise after the alarming ride over the crossings at the London end of the station.

At Waterloo they were ushered in at 3pm precisely and there rising to meet them was OVB. Any impression that the man who could design a 'Merchant Navy' might be in the same mould as Webb or Drummond were quickly dispelled as he was instead quietly spoken, very courteous and put one at ease immediately. He smiled about Basingstoke, but the young Click thought better than to mention the holes in the casing. Framing him behind his desk was a very large photo of 21C3 in works grey but what was even more apparent was a large, all-black wooden model of a Pacific in the Austerity style and of similar outline to the 'Q1'. JGC admits he was drawn to it, thinking it the epitome of a wartime engine: very ugly, yet thoroughly purposeful. He was to learn later it was an early version of the lightweight Pacific later to emerge, better dressed, as the 'West Country' class. Mr Bulleid asked, slightly disbelievingly, 'Do you really want to join my department?' No response is mentioned in the manuscript but instead he was sent outside while Father and OVB discussed terms. The outcome was that he could enter either as a Premium Apprentice or a Pupil. The less expensive £60 Premium option alone was a great sacrifice for his father so that was the way it had to be. 'Don't worry', Mr Bulleid said, '... they're just the same', seemingly sensing the disappointment which JGC had tried to hide. Then a form had to be got. He rang for assistance without result – even CMEs are seemingly ignored at times. Instead, all three trooped off at a brisk pace along the curving corridor. As if he might have done this every day, OVB stopped at a door which turned out to be a cupboard, dived down to a pigeonhole and came up with the right piece of paper. It was signed back in the office. From that day on and certainly later, JGC was proud to admit he felt himself to be one of OVB's men; indeed, if it were but known then, he was also to follow the man and his work for two decades and more.

Back at Shaftesbury Click senior wrote again to the CME asking if there was any possibility that he could go straight into the Drawing Office. In a few days the reply came back inviting him again to Waterloo, to be interviewed this time by 'my Chief Locomotive Designer, Mr C. S. Cocks'. JGC had hoped luck would be on his side as he comments that due to increased drawing office output in the war one possibility was to take suitable boys straight from school.

He was taken into the Waterloo Drawing Office and introduced to Mr Cocks (CSC) who instantly began the questioning: 'Why d'yer want to come to my Drawing Office?' 'Well,' began Click ... any answer being cut short by a further question. 'What d'yer know about locomotives?' This time the young Click was ready. 'I've been watching the "Merchant Navies".' 'What d'yer think of them?' came next. He replied, 'They're on passenger work now.' 'Oh ARE they ...' responded Cocks, then: 'How does the vacuum brake work?' JGC admits being unprepared but feels he must have given a convincing enough reply for Cocks then yelled 'Joe' at the top of his voice.

Instantly, and almost at the trot, entered W. H. Hutchinson, plainly used to being summoned in this way. Cocks went on, 'Here's a schoolboy who knows how the vacuum brake works!' It was probably wise not to mention he had been using the vacuum brake on a 'K10' the day before in the yard at Semley. Even less appropriate would have been to point out that Semley still possessed a shunting horse and a stable where it

was 'shedded'. Also that it never turned a hair when a 'Merchant Navy' went by only feet away.

'When cun yer start at Brighton?' – a statement rather than a question. 'At Brighton, Sir?' JGC asked. 'There's no room here – yer'll have to go down to Redford – Joe, get him on the phone.' There was a pause of sorts then, 'Is that you Redford – I've got a new lad for you; straight from school. Can yer put him up in that spare bedroom of yours?' Cocks' use of the English language and his pronunciation of certain words was sometimes difficult to follow. Even so, the last was more a command than an enquiry; and that problem was solved. CSC went on, 'Yer to go down to Victoria Street and get yerself a scale rule – and then varnish it. It'll last yer all yer life.' It did. Before commencement, though, there was the medical which this time he passed but deliberately did not mention he was due to have his tonsils out 10 days hence. As it was, he went into hospital, was operated upon and discharged himself early ready to start as a premium fitter's apprentice the following week.

Cocks was to be admired from the very start. He was to lead the various apprentices a merry dance in the months to come – but the tune was definitely Bulleid's. Only years afterwards did JGC come to realise quite how intense the pressure on him must have been at the time.

Soon afterwards he travelled to Brighton to start work but was in fact sent to Ashford.

T. H. Redford, 'Tom', although nobody dreamt of calling him that to his face, had come back from retirement to 'do his bit'. His father had been a leading draughtsman under Billinton in the same office but had got the sack after he had criticised the design of the big 4-6-4 tanks which, when new, had rolled badly. Redford senior, though, had been right, as afterwards the side tanks were cut down internally to lower the centre of gravity and a well tank was added between the frames to make good the water loss – even so he wasn't offered his job back. It was to be hoped it wasn't going to be anything like that under Bulleid and Cocks.

Writing with the benefit of hindsight years later, Click comments that if he had become a 'premium', as indeed had Bulleid years earlier, he would have found it hard to imagine OVB in a similar environment doing repetitive work in a machine shop, for example, saddled perhaps with earning piecework at rates set for far younger boys – a mixed blessing of starting late. We might also imagine his furtive mind questioning absolutely everything he came across and wanting to make changes right, left and centre and his frustration at having no power (then) to do anything about it.

At the same time as recounting his own life, Click also affords a new insight into Bulleid's early days in engineering with mention that the young OVB read widely, studied hard and got out and about so much that his workmates must have got very tired of saying 'where's that young Bulleid: he's missing again!', only to get a first-hand account next day of practices at Crewe in the last twilight of Webb's long reign there, or of Holden's 'Decapod's 'superb acceleration' when he sought out that steam challenger to electrification on the Great Eastern. To be honest, we don't know if OVB even saw

Staff in the Brighton Drawing Office, this type of work being JGC's preferred – although unsuccessful – choice when first joining the railway.
Howard Butler collection

this 0-10-0 tank but he would certainly have studied the design from the published drawings, approved of its aims, its huge boiler, its total adhesion concept and its three cylinders. However, with its weight concentrated on such a short wheelbase and its very limited coal and water capacities it quickly began to look far less attractive.

Of Paget's even more extraordinary 'private venture' mixed traffic locomotive being designed in the evenings at Derby he would have heard little or nothing – that would have to wait 30 years or more. Bulleid also studied the GNR Moguls bought from Baldwin's which apparently intrigued him. He studied their drawings intently, appreciated their good points and saw for himself what needed doing to them as they came in for repairs.

For Click, apprenticeship at Ashford was to commence by attacking a great pile of brake hangers which had to have hardened steel bushes force-fitted into them by hand. Perhaps it was the need for a proper convalescence, perhaps it was the simple shock of several things combined but, whatever the cause, by late afternoon on that very first day he passed out, and found himself given a ticket back to Shaftesbury. Despair quickly set in, as he admits himself: it seemed as if nobody could help and there was no future.

To be continued …

Southern Ways and Means

Jeffery Grayer recalls a 1931 publication for the Southern Railway featuring the combined talents of leading British cartoonist 'Fougasse' and writer E. P. Leigh-Bennett.

The Southern Railway, placing great store in the value of publicity not only to attract customers to its services but to deflect some of the criticism levelled at the railway, made effective use of its publicity department. The General Manager of the SR, Sir Herbert Walker, appointed John Elliot to the position of Public Relations Officer, reporting directly to him in 1925. This is generally accepted as being the first occasion that the term PR had ever been used in the UK and under Elliot's stewardship the department blossomed, promoting the 'Southern Electric' brand. After a spell as Deputy General Manager Elliot went on to supersede Missenden as General Manager of the Southern, then becoming Chief Regional Officer of the Southern Region, and later, after having been knighted, he became Chairman of the Railways Executive and then of London Transport. In his capacity as PR guru John Elliot employed the services of author Ernest Pendarves Leigh-Bennett in many publications, amongst the most famous of which were the guidebooks such as *Devon & Cornish Days* and *Come Abroad with Us*, *Golf in the South*, a book on golf courses served by the SR, and the monthly magazine for season ticket holders entitled *Over the Points*. When Leigh-Bennett teamed up with cartoonist Cyril Kenneth Bird, who used

the pen name Fougasse, a unique publication resulted in the shape of *Southern Ways & Means*.

Cyril Bird, or 'Fougasse' as he styled himself, was perhaps to become best known for his wartime posters such as 'Careless Talk Costs Lives', working unpaid for the Ministry of Information for which he was awarded the CBE in 1946, and as contributor to, and later art editor of, *Punch* magazine from 1937, later becoming its editor from 1949 to 1953. He also designed many posters for London Underground.

Several of the freelance contributors to Punch supplemented their income by producing publicity material for the Big Four railway companies. Bird had been seriously wounded during the First World War in the Gallipoli campaign and was invalided out of the Army. His pen name 'Fougasse' derived from a type of anti-personnel mine noted for its erratic performance; he claimed that his art, along with the mine, sometimes hit the spot and sometimes did not! His drawing style evolved from the traditionally representational to an innovative, spare, form that was unique and is well demonstrated in the illustration on the front cover of *Southern Ways & Means* which features a city gent, with his railway ticket clutched in his mouth, laden with parcels, an umbrella and briefcase, all conveyed by a few dextrous strokes of the pen.

Southern Ways & Means, first published in 1931 at a cost of 6d (2.5p), ran to 88 pages with 16 pages of advertisements and consisted of a factual, albeit rather whimsical, text covering over 50 different aspects of the services provided by the Southern interspersed with a number of amusing drawings to illustrate some of the items covered. Reading this nearly 90 years on one is struck not only by the wealth and variety of services once offered by the SR but also by the many changes in the fabric of society in the ensuing years. In short, this publication harks back to a more genteel, refined age than the contemporary one we now find ourselves inhabiting. Dipping into its pages we come across the following gems, referring to a level of service unimaginable to the present-day rail passenger.

The SR offered no fewer than nine different ways of escaping 'from the humdrumming of England'. In short – Dover-Calais characterised as the 'quick way for the man who does not see eye to eye with the Channel' – Folkestone-Boulogne where 'magnificent adventures, like the Bombay Express to Marseilles are disclosed from the quayside' – Newhaven-Dieppe where 'coming home this way by the day service a very pleasant interlude indeed is the cold roast beef of England the moment you get on board particularly after so many French meals!' – Dover-Ostend, the obvious route to 'those 40 miles of Belgian bathing beaches and the excellent holiday golf courses immediately behind the dunes' – Southampton-Havre described as the 'business man's way to Paris', involving departure from Waterloo at 9pm and travelling all night, yet leaving the 'business faculties unimpaired for work at the destination' – Southampton-Caen with trains leaving Waterloo in the afternoon according to the tides – Southampton-St Malo for Dinard and the Brittany coast which is where, according to Leigh-Bennett, 'the English have to a great extent taken over this part of the world for perpetual residence which is not surprising' – Southampton-Channel Islands: 'By night from Waterloo reaching these delicious islands in time for breakfast' – and finally Gravesend-Rotterdam, dining on board one of the Batavier Line ships which have maintained a service between England and Holland since 1830. After dinner one could 'smoke a cigar on deck watching the fascinating night sights of the Thames estuary before turning in'. One could even reserve a special stateroom for the princely sum of £1. Such were the options available to the continental traveller in 1931.

Sending luggage abroad could be fraught with difficulty as, although some countries allowed free baggage, in most there were charges calculated on gross weight. Baggage registration at Victoria was required for all luggage deemed too large to travel in a carriage and it was recommended that registration was done well in advance of the train's departure and on no account should one 'send your chauffeur or valet with the luggage unless he has all your tickets and he is instructed clearly as to which route you would be using'. As an example, if you were travelling to Venice by the Orient Express with a couple

Perhaps Leigh-Bennett's most famous publication is *Devon and Cornish Days* describing West Country holiday spots from Padstow to Charmouth with illustrations by Leonard Richmond.

of heavyish suitcases the charges would be calculated thus:

Gross weight	100lb
Free Allowance	66lb
Excess	34lb

Which would cost you £1 14s 8d made up of the following –

Italian tax	3d
Registration fee	2s
Excess in France	12s 6d
Gross Swiss & Italian (no free allowance)	16s 3d
Handling charge Calais	4d
Italian Customs	8d
Train de luxe	2s
Calais tax	8d

A fascinating section concerns items on which you must pay customs duty. Included, bizarrely, are the following:

Field and opera glasses
Wireless valves
Magnetos and other parts of motor cars and motor cycles
Saccharin
Fire arms, ammunition and explosives!
Opium, cocaine, morphine, heroin, hashish!!

Imagine waiting at a customs desk to have your cases chalk marked carrying some of the above!

Southern Railway employees were to be found at some of the larger continental stations such as the Gare du Nord and

Parlez-vous Franglais?

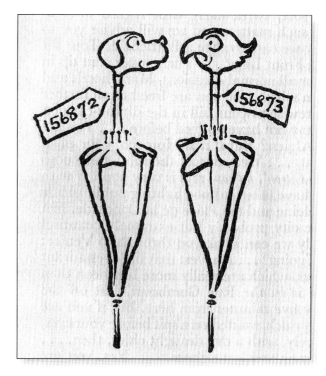

Victim to Lost Property Attendant: 'Yes an umbrella: you'll know it at once: it's got a brown crook and an India-rubber ring round it: the ferrule is a bit worn too.'

Gare St Lazare in Paris, Brussels, Basle, Cologne and Havre who would act as interpreters and who were 'at the disposal of passengers without payment at any time – what the passengers chooses to give them is entirely at his option.'

The SR had a fleet of over 30 passenger ships and 25 cargo steamers plying regularly between the mainland, the continent and the Isle of Wight. On all cross-Channel steamers you could send a wireless telegram for 3½d a word to anywhere in the UK. The SS *Autocarrier* operating between Dover and Calais could carry 35 cars at a time, all of which were stored under cover 'obviating the possibility of salt water damaging fabric or enamelled bodies'. There was also a conveniently placed Chauffeurs' Saloon on the car deck. 'London motorists with chauffeurs can send the man down with their car and leave Victoria by the Ostend morning boat train.'

The Continental Enquiry Office handled all sorts of enquiries, some typical examples being the following:

> 'A man wants a ticket to Peking and his exact route and timing are handed to him within a quarter of an hour. There is a lovely snag when the clerk working it out reaches Harbin because between there and Moscow there is a difference of 6 hours in the clock. But he knows that and merely smiles.'
>
> 'A dear old lady desires to send her cat to Constantinople.'
>
> 'A disquieted lady has her age down on her passport as 40 and in reality she is 50 – do they think it will matter?'

Apparently passengers suffer from two misapprehensions regarding lost property. The first is that if you leave your purse in the train it has inevitably 'gone'. During the past year some £1,500 in loose cash and in purses was handed in to the Waterloo Lost Property Office giving the lie to this assumption. Secondly it is often felt that railway officials will be apathetic on hearing of a passenger's loss. But apparently 'they will become actively interested immediately. Very sleuths they are on these occasions. For instance if a local stationmaster down the line is advised of a loss he at once circularises every station up the line at which the train has stopped.' Quite a service!

There were some very obscure exceptions to the luggage allowance given to certain types of passenger in a carriage. Whilst a first class ticket holder was allowed personal luggage up to 150lb in weight, shipwrecked mariners (how many of those were there likely to be?) were allowed only 56lb of personal luggage, merchant seaman were allowed 168lb but church bell ringers allowed 1½cwt.

A family, or fellow travellers who may have formed themselves into a 'family' whilst on the journey, could obtain private motor omnibuses at Victoria and Waterloo by sending a porter to the Omnibus Office. Costs were 12s 6d for up to three miles and 4s for every mile thereafter. Passengers travelling from the continent to the Midlands, North or West of England would find motor saloons waiting to convey them and their luggage to King's Cross and Marylebone for LNER stations and to Paddington for GWR stations.

Train boards and indicators often confused the traveller and every day many travellers approached the man in charge of the giant indicator boards at London termini to enquire if they were 'right'. 'An unfair stigma,' says Leigh-Bennett, who goes on to explain the workings of the indicator boards thus – 'The internal mechanism of a big Train Indicator consists of a thicket of steel rods which drop into holes punctured in a card, each hole representing a particular station. The man in charge merely has to place the card he wants on a slab, press a lever, and down come the piercing rods. When they don't find a hole they rest placidly on the card and a station, which the train is passing through without stopping, is thus blanked out of the indicator.' It is noted that curiously upon being told that their section of the train is the 'front portion' many passengers immediately make for the rear portion because they see a locomotive against the buffers at the near end of the platform and jump to the conclusion that this is the front of the train whereas of course this locomotive has merely brought the empty carriage stock into the correct platform.

In these current days of 'disability access awareness' it is sobering to recall the concept of Invalid Saloons. A person recovering from an illness or a permanent invalid could be accommodated in special invalid saloons of which there were two types. Firstly there was a complete carriage 'comprising a saloon in the centre with armchairs, tables and a couch for which, if required, a wooden bedstead with spring mattress and well-aired sheets and pillows can be substituted.' The remainder of the carriage consists of a first and a third class compartment and a lavatory. A second type of invalid carriage is also a complete coach but on a smaller scale and lacking corridor connections to the remainder of the train. Each passenger is required to pay the appropriate fare for the class of compartment used with the total amount payable being not less than the sum of four first class and four third class fares with an additional 15s being payable for bed and bedding if required.

Other items, now long lost to carriage by the railways, were the transport of theatrical scenery and effects. In the summer season the SR dealt with some 80 theatrical touring companies each weekend. Special trucks were provided for scenery, being over 50 feet in length and over eight feet high from floor to roof. Innumerable 'special rates' are laid down for the carriage of a multiplicity of items – for example certain itinerant musicians apparently mount a gramophone apparatus on a perambulator which they take to race meetings, where they set them up on the road approach to the racecourse. They are permitted to travel 15 miles with this apparatus by paying 1s 6d but if they send it unaccompanied the cost is 3s, but a pram thus unencumbered travels the same distance for 1s. Travellers with a rickshaw (again can there have been many of these to justify a special rate?) can travel 100 miles for 5s 6d but sending it on ahead costs 11s. Ice cream barrows, knife grinding machines and harps all have a special tariff in this age before simplification and standardisation of goods rates.

Once the traveller had reached his seaside destination there were often Railway Information Bureaux right in the centre of town or on the seafront relieving the passenger of the necessity for travelling back to the station, which Leigh-Bennett admits was often placed 'at the back of the town somewhere', for information. During the summer season these offices are 'thronged with inquirers all day long and there is nothing to pay for this assistance' which helps to answer such questions – all apparently genuine examples – as:

What time do the Fol de Rols start their next show?
What is the name of that pink flower in the Rock Gardens?
Can you find me a good home for the dog for one night, please?

Weather reports were provided outside the Victoria (Continental Side) Baggage Registration Office giving details of the weather and state of the Channel crossing. 'For people to whom a bad crossing is a really serious matter, this is useful information. Except in the height of the very busy season, when seat reservations should not be lightly discarded, you can always send a messenger to Victoria if you live reasonably close to ascertain the state of affairs before making a decision as to whether or not you make the crossing that day.'

The usefulness and economy of season tickets are explained in some detail as is the fact that you could deposit your season ticket, during periods of non-use such as holidays or illness, for a minimum period of 28 days in the expectation of gaining an allowance equivalent to 75% of the unused value. Seasons were even available for dogs such that 'Several dogs of standing would have you know that they have been Southern season ticket holders for some time. Having a great deal in common with their masters and being excruciatingly bored all day in a cat-less garden they saw no valid reason why they should also not come up to the office every day.'

'Gala Trains' is the title given by Leigh-Bennett to the section on the named expresses of the SR. Several are highlighted such as the 'Golden Arrow', the 'Southern Belle' (forerunner of the 'Brighton Belle'), the 'Bournemouth Belle', the 'Bournemouth Limited', the 'City Limited', the 'Sunny South Express', the 'Eastbourne Limited' and the 'Atlantic Coast Express'. Mentioning the competition that led a guard of the SR to win the prize for naming the 'ACE', Leigh-Bennett wonders whether he had the significance of the initial letters in mind when he came up with name but 'it is certainly an ACE of trains. Notice its named portions and the lovely country they cover: Exmouth,

Illustration for the 'Heating in Carriages' section.

Illustration for the 'Go as you please' section devoted to ramblers and an apparently 'hairy kneed' pipe-smoking hiker!

Sidmouth, Seaton, Torrington, Ilfracombe, Padstow, Bude, Plymouth. Realise that each of the coaches costs about £2,000 to build. Put the huge "Lord Nelson" engine at about £12,000, and you will see about £34,000 worth of modern rolling stock, weighing altogether about 450 tons, moving sedately out of Waterloo every morning on the tick of eleven, first stop Salisbury, eighty-four miles, getting there in ninety minutes.'

Predating the plethora of commercial outlets that often swamp modern day stations, Leigh-Bennett mentions 'Station Side-Shows', by which he means to draw attention to the variety of opportunities to spend money whilst hanging about for a train. The bookstall along with the Refreshment Room are obvious examples which have for long been an integral presence at stations. Other facilities mentioned include the telephone, in those wonderful days before the insidious mobile made its appearance, and the telegram office. The great railway hotels adjacent to London termini such as the Grosvenor at Victoria and the Charing Cross Hotel are also mentioned as oases of calm where recently arrived travellers from the Empire can relax and where it would not be long before you 'saw a face that you last saw out there'. You would think that 'with the proximity of Victoria to so many shops that people would not want to shop in the station itself but they do and the monthly volume of business is tremendous.' There is apparently an automatic machine in Victoria station that takes more money than any other in London. The author stood for an hour within visual range of Kelly's Directory and was amazed. 'It sits upon its little lectern on the edge of the main stream of passengers – open to all and free. No wonder its corners are thumbed brown with constant page turning.' The

joys of the pre-internet age! Flowers, for those visiting a convalescent home or more terminally perhaps a cemetery, are available. 'A man in the precincts of the station will not only sell you a perfectly good cabin trunk but an entire wardrobe of clothes to fill it.' Tobacconists do good trade, in those days before health warnings, as do confectioners, chemists, jewellers, and hairdressers.

In addition to having many circular tours of their own available, such as that encompassing the cathedral cities of Canterbury, Rochester, Winchester and Salisbury which could be had for 30s 3d third class, the SR would quote you a price for a circular tour of your own devising. Special trains to visit the liners in Southampton Docks, with fares priced at 7s 6d with luncheon and tea cars included in the train, and to the railway works at Ashford, Eastleigh and Lancing, were also available. These works are 'where 7,000 wagons, 530 locomotives and 2,500 carriages are repaired in a year. Overhead travelling cranes lifting "Lord Nelson" and "King Arthur" engines as easily as you lift a pencil. Pullman cars slung in the air while their undergears are being renovated. Enormous steam hammers punching blocks of steel. Train wheels being turned on great lathes. Huge springs being tested. In fact all the heterogeny of intensive railway manufacture.'

Still much discussed today, and often still not fully implemented, is the co-ordination of rail and road. Back in 1931 the SR had its eye firmly on this ball and did much to dispel 'the alleged fight between the Railway and the Motor Coach Company', stating that it was 'to a great extent a myth. On the contrary we have formed a friendly alliance and are actually working together for the public weal.' Many schemes had been implemented such that 'not only does the bus in many cases come into the station yard but it also serves the little towns and villages that hitherto the railway, with all the will in the world, could not quite reach.' Co-ordination was not just limited to rail and road however, for you could take a

Fishermen could benefit from a scheme that allowed a return journey for the price of a single ticket. Similarly, yachtsmen could journey to Southampton by train to pick up their boat, sail to Poole and return from there by train, paying only the difference between the two fares, if any. Workmen's tickets, available for travel with arrival at the destination station before 8am, were a feature that lingered long into BR days, particularly in the South Wales coalfields, where such tickets and often dedicated trains were run for coalminers.

parcel to 30 of the principal stations on the SR and 'send it to Ootacamund (beloved of the English in the days of the Raj) via Karachi, for example by a combined rail and air route – in fact to anywhere in the world where Imperial Airways or one of their associated companies fly.'

A surprising feature, especially in the current climate of child safety awareness, was the facility to place unaccompanied children in the care of a guard as shown below.

46. Children in charge of Guard

A lady once brought a child to the man at the platform barrier with a label hung round its neck marked 'Eastbourne'. It was under three years of age, she said, and so did not, of course, require a ticket, but could travel free, and would he please pass it on to the Guard? No, she was not travelling with it. And, what is more, the child had come down from Scotland, labelled, alone, and free of cost. Apart from the barrier-man's credulity being stretched to breaking point at this alleged laxity in money matters on the part of the Scottish officials, he, being a family man himself, was very properly incensed at the suggestion. But children *can* be, and often are, sent by train in charge of the paternal Guard. Very small children may travel with him in the van. Others in the carriage of their class, the Guard keeping a watchful eye upon them to their destination.

The legendary railway sandwich could not pass without comment from Leigh-Bennett:

'Anyone who shoulders the task of writing about railway catering is faced at the start with the old bogey of the refreshment room sandwich. Where and when had I been sold a stale sandwich? I hadn't. Nor could I quote anyone who had. But the canard had grown up with me as with others. It would be to the advantage of nobody in the management of a Southern buffet to put forward so uneconomic an item of sales. If such a person had perishable stock left over unduly at the end of the day perambulating inspectors would want to know the reason why. The thing that strikes one most forcibly is the clever way in which suppliers have mastered the law of average in consumption. They can tell almost to one bath bun.' As the legend of the stale curly sandwich persisted well into BR days perhaps the author's confidence in the freshness of food items was not entirely well-founded.

Safety being of paramount concern to the railways great stress was laid upon the ability of staff to perform first aid in the event of any mishap. In the Guard's van of all mainline trains there was kept a medical case containing the following items:

1 set splints
1 doz. safety pins
6 triangular bandages
1 roll adhesive plaster
1 pkt cotton wool
1 pair scissors
6 1in roller bandages
2 bottles iodine
6 2in roller bandages
1 bottle sal volatile
6 3in roller bandages
1 bottle smelling salts
1 drinking cup
6 burn dressings
2 pkts lint
1 tourniquet

Under the heading 'Fur Feather and Fin' it is claimed that 'there are very few animals that the Southern does not carry from

time to time. An elephant is, of course, quite a mundane matter with them and one went down to Bournemouth recently in his covered van at the rear of a passenger train.' The animal world has its own tables of rates, rules, safeguarding appliances and rolling stock far too detailed to enumerate individually. Some interesting snippets however were:

'Calves may have the body and legs entirely enveloped in the sack or with the body in and the legs out. Guinea pigs unsold at shows are allowed back to the owner at half the outward rate.' 'An ass travelling with a horse in the same horsebox on the same journey travels with a half fare ticket and presumably with a slight inferiority complex. Sea lions, tigers and ostriches go at specially arranged rates which seems only reasonable and expedient.' Circus movements by train are second nature to the Southern and it is usually an all-night job for railway staff. Take for example a circus moving from Winchester to Exeter. 'The circus proprietor asks to be moved these 118 miles after the last performance on Saturday night. Everything must be reassembled in its pomp and panoply in time for the first show in Exeter on Monday afternoon. An exact description of the traffic is obtained – what wild animals and how many. Weight of elephants. Inventory of all show gear. Exact nature and number of vehicles. Decision as to loading and unloading. Yard accommodation. Craneage powers. In what order consignments are to be brought. How many special trains and their timing etc. The elephants are generally most accommodating in

the matter of their carriages – they do the knees-bend business and crawl into a covered van raising themselves benevolently when snugly inside. The largest of the 12 circuses normally touring the country takes usually about 110 passengers and 40 vehicles of various descriptions needing two complete special trains every time it moves.' The number of circuses touring the UK these days certainly bears no relationship to those operating in the 1930s and they no longer use animals in their shows and they certainly do not use the railways for transport. Like so many other items in this brief survey this is just another aspect of life nearly 90 years ago that has changed out of all recognition.

Southern Ways & Means was printed by the prestigious Curwen Press of Plaistow, East London. The firm had been founded by the Reverend John Curwen in 1863 to publish sheet music for the 'tonic sol-fa' system. Under the management of the founder's grandson the Curwen Press was at the vanguard of the design revolution that saw expression in British printing in the early 20th century and many well-known graphic artists, including Eric Ravilious and Paul Nash, worked with Curwen. The Press's output included books, posters and published ephemera and in 1977 the Tate Galley held an exhibition called Artists at Curwen: A Celebration of the Gift of Artists' Prints from the Curwen Studio. Although the sheet music division became independent in 1930 and the Curwen Press closed in 1984 the Curwen Studio still survives today as an independent design studio.

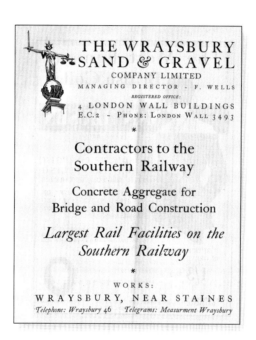

One of the advertisers in *Southern Ways & Means* with a close connection to the SR.

Tailpiece from the rear cover – the satisfied SR passenger (hopefully!).

Lynton & Barnstaple Revisited

Stephen Phillips

One of the more unusual lines to become part of the Southern Railway at the Grouping in 1923 was the narrow gauge Lynton & Barnstaple Railway in North Devon. Commencing at Barnstaple Town on the ex-LSWR Ilfracombe branch, the 1ft 11½in gauge Lynton line climbed some 19¼ miles to the terminus at Lynton, perched 700 feet above the twin village of Lynmouth on the rugged North Devon coast. The summit of the line was reached at the wind swept Woody Bay station at almost 1,000 feet above sea level. The view of Woody Bay dates from circa 1924. It is difficult to tell at first glance that this is a Southern Railway period view. Little had changed since the independent L&B period and the Southern faced an immediate backlog of maintenance including fencing, track, signalling, locomotives and rolling stock. Track in this view is laid on little more than squared-off untreated logs in weed clogged ballast, with the original 42lb flat-bottomed rails clearly cutting into the rotten timber, dog spiked with bolts and clips only at the joints. Original Evans O'Donnell signalling equipment is still in use, the starting signal having been shortened over the years as the base of the wooden post rotted. This signal would eventually be replaced with a SR rail-built signal. Point rodding is carried in Evans Patent rollers. The Southern undertook a complete relaying of the track, and complete re-fencing of the line in the mid-twenties, introducing concrete sleepers on certain straight lengths of track. In this view the telegraph poles have been replaced with concrete posts. The station master Oliver Mills' dog keeps an eye on proceedings as American Baldwin-built 2-4-2T *LYN* prepares to depart for Lynton with a train comprising an original Bristol-built brake van, coupled to open-centre, observation brake and third class carriages. *LYN* had been built in May 1898 at Baldwin's factory in Philadelphia (builder's No 15965). At the time she was the only American-built locomotive on the Southern. She lasted until the line closed in 1935 and would be overhauled at Eastleigh in 1928/29. That she wasn't scrapped when *LEW* was purchased in 1925 suggests that she was regarded as a useful asset. Southern Railway cast brass oval number plates have been attached to the cab sides in this view, displaying her new Southern Railway number as E762, displacing her nameplates to the tanks. Her chimney is a Urie-style stovepipe which replaced her original copper-capped BLW stack in 1922. In the distance a coal wagon has been left in the siding, to be unloaded by the local coal merchant. The sheds in the distance were used to store manures (fertilizer) and feeds, distributed to local farmers. Beyond the last carriage, the line falls away at 1 in 50 towards Barnstaple. To the right of the train, the gas pipe fence carries the usual period enamel advertising signage from which the railway derived a modest income. The well-known nationwide brand of Sutton's Seeds appeared at several L&B stations. Less well known is the more local dark blue enamelled advert for W. Brock & Co. of Exeter (upper right). The contemporary magazine advert (right) captures the period well. © *Reginald S. Clark/Rail Archive Stephenson*

Photographed from the road overbridge (No 69 Martinhoe Cross Bridge) immediately north of Woody Bay station, *LEW* enters the cutting and heads for Lynton with a mixed train circa 1927/8. A number of Southern Railway improvements are visible; track has been relaid with new sleepers, clipped and bolted and re-ballasted. New locomotive *LEW* (Manning, Wardle & Co, Leeds, 1925/2042) is in full Maunsell olive green livery and a new 8-ton covered van built in 1927 by J. & F. Howard of Bedford is the second vehicle in the train, behind L&B 8-ton bogie open wagon No 22 (renumbered SR No 28313 in February 1933). The wagon has not yet been repainted in SR livery, nor has it received enamelled signs warning against overloading with ballast. Clearly, during the track overhauls it was possible to unintentionally overload these wagons with the new ballast which was being sent up from Meldon Quarry. To prevent this, an iron strip was fitted inside the open bogie wagons, approximately half way up the sides, to indicate the weight limit of ballast loading. No 22 was built by the L&B company at Pilton Works in 1903. It appears to be loaded here with house coal bound for Lynton. Coal for Lynmouth continued to be loaded on to the beach direct from sailing vessels from South Wales as this was more convenient (and cheaper) than hauling it down from Lynton. The Howard van was one of four new vans built to SR Diagram 1456, numbered 47042-47045. At the same time, J. & F. Howard also built four new 8-ton bogie open wagons. Originally built with ash frames, external timber X-bracing and deal boarding, these vans were well used but did not weather well once water started collecting in the joints when the flashing was compromised; consequently, modifications in 1934 saw them rebuilt with steel bracing and smooth planked sides. Above the cutting can be seen the roof of the Woody Bay Hotel. The tall up home signal in the distance is an original Evans O'Donnell example. Woody Bay station was originally called Wooda Bay, and was intended to serve the nearby Woody Bay which early promoter Colonel Benjamin Lake had hoped to develop into a resort. A pier was built to enable pleasure steamers to call there but it was not accessible at low tides (the Bristol Channel has one of the greatest tidal ranges in the world). In 1899 the pier partially collapsed in a storm, eventually being scrapped entirely in 1902. Plans to develop the area did not come to fruition, and Colonel Lake went bankrupt, leaving Woody Bay station as one of the highest and most isolated stations on the Southern system. *© W. V. Wiseman/Rail Archive Stephenson*

EXE (Manning, Wardle 2-6-2T SR No E760) enters Woody Bay on 5 August 1935. Note the coal merchant's weighing scales alongside a Howard bogie open wagon. To the left of the photograph can be seen part of the replacement SR rail-built LQ signal with another visible above the carriage roof. A number of other SR improvements are also visible including concrete sleepers and external point locking bars. When the SR relaid the track, much of the original rail, switches and crossings, locks (some economic), detectors, rodding and rollers installed by Evans O'Donnell in 1898 were re-used. Originally locking bars were fitted inside, but the SR repositioned them outside with the overhanging tyre tread profile preventing the bar from being lifted. Additional ex-LSWR equipment was also brought up from Exeter. New treated sleepers replaced the old worn out and rotten L&B timber, clogged and dirty ballast was completely replaced with new high-quality free draining Meldon ballast, and rails were fixed by clips and fang bolts at every sleeper sitting on new steel bed-plates, resulting in more resilient track. Super-elevation was also introduced, following best main line practice. *G.N. Southerden/Author's collection*

Taken by W. V. Wiseman on the same date as the previous Wiseman view, circa 1927/8, from the New Mill Lane overbridge (No 75) which survives today immediately north of Caffyns Halt. *YEO* (SR No E759, Manning, Wardle & Co, 1897) approaches Caffyns Halt from Lynton with a short mixed train comprising a new Howard van, a 4-wheel open and two bogie carriages. *YEO* is in Maunsell lined olive green livery, but does not have the Southern lettering or large number on the tanks and bunker. Instead the SR oval number plate is carried on the bunker side and the tank side name plate occupies its original (on) position. The track here does not look like it has yet been relaid and is overgrown with grass and weeds; at the boundary the stock-proof fencing is original L&B wood post type, not yet replaced with SR concrete post and wire. The remains of the wooden 17½ milepost rest on the ground alongside the engine. Livestock (typically sheep) would often get on to the line and any losses would result in a claim by the farmer, hence secure fencing and gates were a priority when the SR took responsibility for the line. At least one concrete telegraph pole has been erected. In the far distance the line curves left under the main road to Lynton (overbridge No 76 Dean Steep) which runs behind the hedge on the left. Many of the road bridges featured dog-leg approaches and were rather hazardous for motorists. When the L&B closed in 1935 the local authorities straightened out many of the roads affected by filling in the cuttings and removing the bridges and earthworks. The roof and chimney visible on the horizon is a former isolation hospital. Caffyns Halt existed as an un-named platform c1904, eventually receiving a shelter in 1912. Its primary role was to serve the nearby golf course which had opened on nearby Caffyns Heanton Down in 1895. © W. V. Wiseman/Rail Archive Stephenson

Golf.—Lynton Golf Club, 9-hole course (2,513 yards) on Caffins Down, two miles from Lynton, and 1,000 feet above sea level. Train from Lynton to Golf Siding, 6d. return. Cab fare from Lynton, 3/-. Subscription, 21/- per year, visitors, 10/- per month, 6/- per fortnight, 4/- per week, 1/- per day. No introduction fee. Fuller particulars can be had from the Hon. Sec., Mr. Kingsland Jutsum.

By the early 1920s the internal combustion engine was beginning to have an impact on the railway as a means of transport to Lynton. The end of the war had provided a supply of surplus lorries together with imports of affordable reliable and powerful American vehicles from Chevrolet and Ford. After closure, Pickfords were quick to offer a replacement service for luggage, goods and parcels. *Both author's collection*

Blackmoor station circa 1935. Blackmoor was one of the larger stations on the L&B, situated at a busy crossroads. A large livestock auction took place regularly and the auction site is clearly seen behind the hotel. The hotel grew out of an earlier cafe which served the busy auction; eventually it was rebuilt in 1930 in Art Deco style by Jimmy Broom, and this photo postcard was taken for publicity purposes. Fortunately the photographer, Barnstaple-based R. L. Knight, captured the station buildings. Lynton is to the left in this view. Although the auction was very popular, little livestock was carried by the railway, with most of it arriving by road. Roads were free, and in this part of Devon the high banked lanes were ideal for driving livestock. Barnstaple market trains were also popular with farmers. One old farmer recalled an argument between farmers on the returning train one late evening as to whether there were two full moons shining over North Devon, such was the convoluted route of the line. The hotel burned down in 1970 and the station today is a restaurant. *Author's collection*

Crews pose for the photographer as their double-headed train waits at Chelfham as trains cross, August 1935. E762 *LYN* with wooden cab and E760 *EXE* in immaculate condition are seen with only a few weeks remaining until closure. The Southern did its best to keep the line going; sadly it was not to be. *G. N. Southerden/ Author's collection*

Robert Billinton's Brighton 4-4-0s

Jeremy Clarke

Robert Billinton's career as the Locomotive Superintendent of the London, Brighton & South Coast Railway was one of mixed fortune. His range of 0-6-2 'radial' tank engines was in general excellently matched to the work for which they were designed. Some other classes tended to be under-boilered, however, a not unusual failing among locomotive engineers made elsewhere at the time. The fact that, other than the 'E6' class, all the 'radials' as well as the 'C2' class 0-6-0 goods engines (the 'Vulcans') later had the cylinders reduced in diameter from 18in to 17½in is, perhaps, an indication of that. Billinton's first essay into express passenger locomotives had the same characteristic.

One of the premier classes of express passenger engine in use on the LBSCR at the time of Billinton's arrival at Brighton was the 2-4-0 'Belgravia' class of tender engines. Six were built by Stroudley between 1872 and 1876. The term 'new' is perhaps not strictly accurate as they incorporated the frames for a 2-4-0 designed by Stroudley's predecessor John Craven, whilst two of the class were actually rebuilds of 2-2-2 engines. Whatever, No 201, seen here and named as per the class, originated from one of a pair built in 1872. Initially poor steamers, this was resolved and although it may be hard to imagine a century and more later, they were entrusted with the business express train between Brighton and London Bridge until about 1881. Renumbered 501 in 1897, the engine lasted until February 1899, with the last of the class withdrawn in 1902. The safety valves fitted were sometimes unkindly referred to as of the 'bathing drawers' type.

When Billinton arrived in Brighton from Derby in February 1890 following the untimely death of William Stroudley the previous December, the heaviest main line duties were covered by the inimitable 'B1' class 0-4-2, the 'Gladstones'. Despite the doom-mongers' view that engines with coupled wheels no less than 6ft 6in in diameter leading were inherently dangerous, the only accident involving one (Norwood Junction, 1 May 1891) was caused by a bridge failure and not by the engine. Stroudley was of the opinion in this case that stability as well as maximum adhesion was gained by having the driving wheels under the heaviest part of the engine.

His 'G' class 2-2-2s also had a presence, particularly on the Portsmouth route where they did very well despite the difficult gradients. It has to be said, however, that the loads were relatively light and the timetables did not in general require average speeds much above 40mph. The LSWR's 'Direct Portsmouth' line via Guildford was, as the name implies, shorter than the roundabout route built piecemeal by the Brighton, so competition was more in name than in fact, especially as the two companies had a 'pooling' arrangement for revenue.

Being among the least powerful express engines still in main line use, it was the 'Gs' that Billinton first sought to supersede. The class was a compromise between two singleton 'singles', the beefy *Grosvenor* of 1874 and the dainty *Abergavenny* of 1876.

The first of the 24 genuine examples, No 327, *Imberhorne,* had emerged from Brighton Works in December 1880. The engines were numbered consecutively, the last, No 350, named *Southbourne,* being completed in April 1882. The third in the sequence, No 329, traditionally taking the named *Stephenson* in the Brighton stock lists, was among those in the Stephenson Centenary Procession at Wylam in 1881.

At the time of Billinton's appointment the singles were allocated to New Cross, Battersea, Brighton and Fratton, indicative of their primary duties. The cylinders were 17in x 24in, driving wheels 6ft 6in and the boiler, offering 1,184sq ft of heating surface, was pressed at 140psi, though that later was increased to 150psi. At 85% of that pressure the tractive effort was 11,338lb. The driving axle carried 13½ tons giving a remarkably low adhesion factor of 2.67:1 which makes one wonder at their supposed prowess. Certainly J. N. Maskelyne, who knew them well, if in the twilight of their existence, contends they had 'a very firm grip on the road when running' though there must have been the perhaps inevitable bouts of slipping from time to time, particularly, one assumes, on starting.

Having then completed the outstanding order for Stroudley's 'E1' 0-6-0T, introduced his own 'D3' class 0-4-4T and the class 'C2' 'Vulcan' 0-6-0s, Billinton's replacement for the 'Gs' began to take shape in the form of the 'B Bogie' 4-4-0. The first drawings, completed in October 1892, were effectively of little, if any, advance on the 'G' despite the 'new' wheel arrangement. Modification and enhancement of the specification early the next year were undertaken to make the engine more widely useful. But it was not until two years later that work on the first three of an initial ten was started. No 314, named *Charles C. Macrae* – a Director and later Chairman of the Company – eventually left Brighton Works in June 1895. The second engine, No 315, *Duncannon,* by which title the class was generally known, and 316, *Goldsmid*,* followed in July. The engines weighed 42t 16cwt in working order of which all but 14t was adhesive. The tender held four tons of coal and 2,420 gallons, though those attached to all other class members beyond the first three had a capacity of 2,600 gallons.

One immediate problem concerned the Brighton's turntables, which all but matched the engine's wheelbase of 44ft 6in. Those at the six major depots had therefore to be lengthened.

For the first time Brighton had produced not just an engine with a leading bogie but coupled wheels of 6ft 9in diameter. Certainly driving wheels of that size had been used on Brighton locos before although only on 'singles'. Would wheels of a smaller diameter have been advantageous? The mileage of the Brighton main lines could not compare with those of the Midland Railway, and by implication relatively fast acceleration over the lesser distances between stops that smaller wheels could provide would surely have been beneficial.

The boiler was as applied to Billinton's 'C2' class 0-6-0 goods engine, being only 4ft 3in in diameter, though in later 'B2s' those of 4ft 5in diameter were provided. The engines had, in Hamilton Ellis's words, 'a certain modesty in respect of heating surface'. This was 1,220sq ft in the early boilers, the later ones having about 10% more than this: the grate area in both instances was but 18.73sq ft. Such dimensions made them suitable for hauling an easily-timed freight train

'B2' No 171 *Nevill*, built in June 1897 at a cost of £2,458, is seen here with the 1899 Royal Train. Despite the shortcomings of the type, No 171 ran in excess of 192,000 miles in the five years 1898 to 1902 with a minimum of 27,059 in 1898 and a maximum of 48,660 in 1901. (This despite an incident on 1 February 1900 when the engine was pushed chimney first into the oil store at New Cross when shunting 23 coal wagons. It transpired the sanding gear was defective.) No 171, later 2071, was converted to a 'B2X' in October 1910 and ran a total of 1.4 million miles before being withdrawn from service in May 1931.

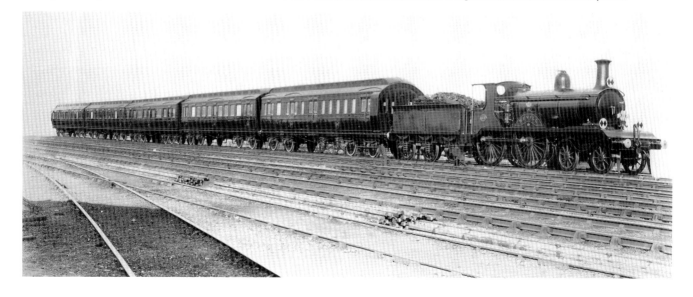

*Goldsmid had been allocated to Billinton 'D3' class 0-4-4T No 363 upon its appearance in May 1892. The engine's outline so pleased the Brighton director, Sir Julian Goldsmid, that it was reproduced as an engineman's cap badge and remained so until Grouping. On losing its name to the new 'B2', No 363 became *Havant*.

'B4' No 54, *La France*, dating from May 1900, was originally named *Empress*. The name *La France* was carried for just nine days in August 1905 when it worked various trains in connection with the Entente Cordiale celebrations. The repainting was undertaken at New Cross and for the period it ran with the tender from No 52, its own tender deemed unserviceable due to badly worn tyres and a leaking tank. Post-August 1905 it reverted to *Empress* but was renamed *Princess Royal* in August 1906. The engine is seen here decorated, in which form it ran a number of journeys in both directions between Victoria and Portsmouth. (In practical terms we may wonder how such decoration on a locomotive – flags, bunting, banners and flags – withstood travel at all but the lowest speeds.)

perhaps, but were hardly enough to sustain the continuous demand of a heavy main line express. Maybe this should not surprise us. Billinton had been Chief Draughtsman at Derby under S. W. Johnson, having gone there from Brighton with Stroudley's encouragement. During his nearly 16 years' service with the Midland it was inevitable he had been imbued with that company's philosophy of running light trains at frequent intervals behind small engines or by double heading if required – labour costs at the time being small. The 'B2' – as the class became under Marsh – was therefore a small engine with a very 'Midlandish' look, elegant and refined, the smokebox crowned by a tall, tapering chimney that subtly curved outwards at the rim, and Salter safety valves at the dome. One gets the impression from all this that Billinton was as much concerned with the look of the engine – another Johnson trait! – as with its usefulness. Besides the novelty of a bogie, Gresham & Craven injectors were fitted too, another Brighton 'first'.

No 314 was put on to the prestigious 8.45am up and 5.0pm return Brighton-London Bridge expresses and failed badly. One might have understood even an experienced crew, handling for the first time a brand new and unfamiliar engine, finding perhaps a little difficulty in maintaining the timetable. But time was lost consistently throughout all the journeys and coal consumption proved rather heavier than that of the 'B1' class, the 'Gladstones', which had run the train happily and economically for years. It has to be said, however, that the B2 class was dimensionally superior and, in tractive effort terms, marginally more powerful too, all rather puzzling anomalies; the more so, since the new 4-4-0 was supposedly set, in time, to supersede the 'B1' on the heavier services. Moreover, the engine rode very roughly with some quite disturbing 'hunting', especially on tangent track. These failings seem odd given Billinton's considerable experience at the drawing board. In view of his length of service with the Midland it is inconceivable the company would have tolerated poor steaming and continuing rough riding in the many 4-4-0s produced during his time at Derby without seeking a lasting solution. The question is what had he done differently here that apparently so contrasted with established Midland practice?

Modifications were made to the dampers, ashpan and the blastpipe of the three in an attempt to improve combustion and steaming, leading to further tests being made on the Portsmouth line with No 316. Coal consumption still proved excessive, some 20% more than the 'singles' consumed with comparable loads. Perhaps as a consequence this engine was the first of the class to have the cylinders lined-up to 17½in diameter.

Despite all the problems Billinton ordered another eight which came into traffic in the last six months of 1896 with the numbers 317-324. These merely emphasised how even the enlarged version of his first essay to supersede the 'singles' was simply not up to the task. Nevertheless, another 14, Nos 171 and 201-213, emerged from Brighton between March and December 1897. The last of these, named *Bessemer,* had a larger boiler still, though only increased in diameter to 4ft 8in: all else mechanically remained unchanged. Despite containing no less than 1,464.82sq ft of surface and a grate of 20½sq ft the engine was still under-boilered. Marsh tinkered with it, providing new cylinders and reclassifying it 'B3'. Performance still remained disappointing.

Billinton turned his attention in 1898 to countering the rough riding, mainly by redistributing the weight and tightening the bogie springs. The results were not much of an improvement. And the rough riding revealed another weakness soon after the engines entered service. Cracks began to appear in the frames at their shallowest point, where they passed over the driving axles. None of the 25 escaped additional plating being added to strengthen these weak spots, quite heavily in some cases. It may be something of a surprise then to find that the class as a whole ran very high annual mileages, four of them having got more than a million miles to their credit by Grouping.

Was it a test to see if the changes instituted in 1898 had been successful when, on 2 October that year, No 206, *Smeaton* (entered service 5/97) had charge of the first 'Sunday Pullman Limited'? The train consisted of five Pullman Cars and two accumulator vans – 'Pullman Pups' – a tare load of about 180 tons for the first official 'Brighton in one Hour' attempt. It has to be assumed in view of the class's poor reputation the engine was specially selected and prepared; very possibly the crew too, no doubt particularly experienced, skilled, and perhaps fearless men being allocated the duty. Seemingly, the train made it to Brighton in the allotted time.

A year after this event No 206 was involved in a serious accident at Wivelsfield when, in dense fog, she ran into the rear of a preceding train. There were eight fatalities. No 206 was also seriously damaged, all axles except the trailing coupled one being broken as was the front buffer beam, the smokebox and much of the footplating. Though the blame was placed principally on the driver, the Inspecting Officer, Col Sir Francis Marindin, made some very caustic remarks about the company's signalling infrastructure and regulations; in the case of the latter particularly those concerned with fog working.

In view of their initial purpose the first dozen 'B2's went to Fratton and soon usurped the 'singles' on the best Portsmouth expresses. As has been noted already, the crews were unimpressed and it was probably the Pompey men who were responsible for coining the 'Grasshopper' nickname, suggested as being due to the nature of the riding. Other class members found themselves on Hastings and Eastbourne main line traffic and a substantial number went to Brighton shed. Some redistribution occurred as time passed but only to sheds which supplied power to these routes though Bognor got a later look in.

There had been little in the way of re-allocation by Grouping but reconstruction and updating of the class had occurred in the meantime under Marsh. The first to undergo the transition to 'B2X' was No 321, the former *John Rennie,* of November 1896. It emerged in new form from Brighton in October 1907 bearing a 'C3' class 0-6-0's boiler of 5ft 0in diameter pressed at 170psi, having a closed dome on the rear of the two rings, Ramsbottom safety valves on the firebox and an extended smokebox on a saddle. Mechanically the engine was unchanged except for the addition of equalizing beams between the coupled axles. This was aimed at counteracting

Prince of Wales in plain umber livery – post May 1906. The names were carried until Southern Railway policy dictated they be removed. Built in September 1902, this engine lasted until June 1936.

the rough riding, a problem that had never been completely solved, and its stress-related effects on the frame. The higher pitch of the boiler also required a new cab. The changes certainly made the engine look more modern but the overall result was still a disappointment, particularly as coal consumption continued to be excessive. Nevertheless, the process continued and was almost complete by the time Marsh resigned on health grounds in 1911. It was left to Billinton the Younger to finish the job with Nos 209 and 324 in April and May 1913, No 319 in June 1914 and No 316 in July 1916. Among other things, in time boilers were provided with Lawson Billinton's top feed and most of the tenders also had a well installed to bring capacity up to 2,985 gallons.

The class lasted through the war years and Grouping but it was the latter that saw them coming to their end. The availability of more efficient – and numerous – contemporary pre-Grouping 4-4-0 engines, particularly from the SECR, which had been released by the influx of new Maunsell Moguls, emphasised how comparatively poorly the 'B2X' performed in everyday service. The first five went in 1929, Nos 208 and 317 in June, 204 in July, and 201 and 316, the former *Goldsmid,* in December. Thereafter things happened quite quickly, the last of the 25, No 206, the racing *Smeaton,* going in March 1933. All the engines had had the Southern's 'B' prefix added to their numbers but it seems only *Smeaton* and No 323, formerly *William Cubitt* (withdrawn 11/32), received the '2000' that superseded it.

Billinton had produced his 'E3' 0-6-2 'radial' tanks and had most of the similar 'E4' 0-6-2 engines in traffic before turning his attention back to a class for express work: the result was the 'B4' 4-4-0. Nos 52-54 emerged from Brighton during the three months December 1899-February 1900. This class turned out to be all that their predecessors were not, though coal consumption still proved to be high with heavy loads.

Cylinders were 18in x26in, the 4ft 10in diameter boiler, pitched 8ft 1½in above the rail, offered 1,509sq ft of surface plus another 126sq ft in the firebox, which held a grate area of 23¾sq ft, and a pressure of 180psi. At the usual 85% of this the tractive effort worked out at 17,729lb. Unlike the cylinders in the 'B2', those of the 'B4' were cast in one piece with the valves beneath them. The coupled wheelbase at 8ft 9in was the same as in the 'B2' but the overall wheelbase came out at 3in more by that addition to the distance between the bogie and the driving axle. Weight in working order was 51½ tons of which 35 tons was adhesive. The tenders in this first three weighed 33t 7cwt and carried six tons of coal and 2,985 gallons.

Were the additional three inches in the wheelbase an attempt to mitigate against the rough riding that plagued the 'B2'? Certainly the 'B4' was never the subject of frequent complaints on that front which suggests the attempt was successful. But the class still suffered from the weak framing over the driving axles that plagued the 'B2', and before long all were similarly plated.

Presumably satisfied with the work of the first three, Billinton ordered another 25 from Sharp Stewart. Numbered 47-51/55-74, these came into service between June and October 1901. There were some differences. The boiler, for example, was pitched 1½in higher than that in the original trio, and was of two rings rather than three, with the dome on the second ring. The tenders weighed two tons more. It was from these engines the class name, 'Scotchmen' was taken, though Maskelyne additionally titles them 'Busters'. For some reason the usual Brighton naming after the second engine into traffic, *Sirdar*, never caught on. Six similar engines, numbered 42-46, came out of Brighton in May and June 1902 to take the total number in traffic to 33.

No E42, the former *His Majesty*, in Southern colours, which had a 45-year life between 1902 and 1947. The location is not reported but could be Bognor.

Whereas the 'B2's had looked to engineers and people connected with the LBSCR for names, the 'B4's mainly ranged over royalty, and personages and places to do with the near-contemporary Boer War. The first engine of the last batch, No 42, was named *His Majesty* and inevitably became the Brighton's Royal engine. It was, incidentally, one of the very few in the class to retain its name until removal by the Southern after Grouping. Among other names we find *Kitchener* (No 58), *Ladysmith* (No 61), *Mafeking* (No 62) and *Pretoria* (No 63). The last four of the Sharp Stewart lot fell back on well-established Brighton names, *Sussex* and *Cornwall*, for example, but then we find prosaic *Bagshot* (No 69) hiding among the great and the good and reminders of South African doings.

When all were in traffic the allocation at first was fifteen at Brighton, seven each at New Cross and Battersea, and two each at Portsmouth and St Leonards.

No 54 *Empress* wrote herself into the history books by making a record run in bringing Queen Victoria's funeral train back to London following the monarch's death at Osborne at the end of January 1901. This was made up of the Brighton's sumptuous Royal train built in 1897 by Robert Billinton for the Prince of Wales, later King Edward VII. Among other things the Prince had given explicit instructions for, there should be no corridor connections anywhere in the train, instructions that were to have an impact on this particular journey. Augmented by similarly sumptuous Pullman carriages and a Great Western Railway Saloon bearing the Queen's body, the train with the substantial mourning party aboard set off from Royal Clarence Yard at Gosport on 2 February at 8.45am. Being Westinghouse-braked it required the services of a dual-fitted LSWR engine to take it to Fareham, where No 54 was waiting. The task fell to Adams 'Jubilee' class 0-4-2 No 555. It was allowed nine minutes to get to Fareham with the engine changeover (and reversal of direction) being scheduled to take four minutes.

Unfortunately, whoever had worked out the seating arrangements had overlooked this reversal of direction at Fareham. Had the carriages been vestibuled correctly this might not have been too difficult. As it was, the necessary changes had to be accomplished by the dignitaries physically leaving the 'wrong' carriage to find and board the correct one, 'status' dictating who should be nearest the front or not. The delay in getting the various parties into their proper places, not helped by the shortness of Fareham's platforms, resulted in departure being 10 minutes late.

In life the Queen had instructed railway staff her train should travel at no more than forty mph – and it was also known she bore a particular dislike for the LBSCR! Perhaps it was as well she now lay coffined in the quietude of her Great Western saloon carriage, for knowing the new King was a stickler for punctuality the company's Outdoor Locomotive Superintendent, J. J. Richardson, who rode on the footplate, urged the driver, Walter Cooper, later one of the Brighton's senior Locomotive Inspectors, to try to make up some of the lost time. It is reported speed along much of the easily graded coast line between Fareham and Arundel Junction was taken at near-80 miles an hour, and some knowing hearts must have

been in several dry mouths with an *estimated* 90mph *apparently* being noted on the long descent from Holmwood towards Dorking, with the sharp curves there either side of Betchworth tunnel. It was as well perhaps the Brighton used the Westinghouse brake. Driver Cooper and Fireman Way, to the King's satisfaction no doubt, brought the train into Victoria at 10.58am, two minutes early.

Whether Billinton took any particular note of some of the 'B4's powers in everyday service is difficult to establish. Whatever the case, he chose No 70 *Holyrood* as his guinea pig for a series of tests of various sorts in December 1902, that engine having already demonstrated its prowess. A few days before Christmas 1901 she went down to Brighton with the Sunday 'Pullman Limited' – now of eight carriages and two 'Pullman Pups', a weight of about 270 tons tare – in 53min 49sec. Was it then some rivalry between crews that saw No 68 *Marlborough* run the train down to the coast on Christmas Day in a time of 51min 11sec with a maximum speed of 88mph recorded at Horley? Whether this level was maintained for a whole year seems doubtful, but Billinton must have been impressed enough by everyday performance to make these tests. The results were reported as producing 'reasonably good figures'. That rather suggests coal consumption was still greater than it ought to have been.

Whatever *Holyrood* may have accomplished in the interim, the highlight of her career came on 26 July 1903. At that time the Brighton company was being 'threatened' with an electric London-Brighton railway line without intermediate stops and the possibility of a 50-minute timing. This idea was not just alarming to the LBSCR's Board but such a competitor over its most prestigious route was an anathema too. In much the same way as Gresley did nearly a quarter century later, Billinton decided to demonstrate what steam could do. The road was specially cleared for the 130-ton tare weight train made up of three 'Pullmans' and a van. *Holyrood* and Driver Tompsett did not disappoint, reaching Brighton in 48min 41sec at an average of 63.4mph start to stop and a maximum of 90mph at Horley. The more difficult return took 50min 20sec, an average of 60.8mph with a maximum of 85mph, again at Horley. It is doubtful this 'showpiece' actually dismayed the electric people but no more was heard of the scheme.

A few name changes featured among the 'B4s', some from quite early on. All three 'prototypes' were so re-christened, No 52, *Siemens,* becoming *Sussex* in September 1908, No 53, *Sirdar,* came to honour *Richmond* in November 1906, and No 54 lost one regal title, *Empress,* for another, *Princess Royal,* in August 1906. No 72, also *Sussex,* retained that title unchanged: the renaming of No 53 is generally accepted as being due to an error in the paintshop, apparently not corrected until the name was erased under the Marsh regime.

No 59, formerly *Baden Powell,* received a Phoenix superheater in May 1912. This was really no more than a glorified steam dryer. It consisted of rings of piping to carry the steam within an extended and enlarged smokebox, which required modifications to the engine's frames and platforms to accommodate it. A success, it seems, it was not, the

Formerly No 60 *Kimberley* is seen here as Southern Railway No 2060 running as a 'B4X', the conversion of which occurred in September 1922. The full SR livery is seen here, being cleaned. This engine later received an 'S' prefix at nationalisation and was painted black. Much of the time post-1948 was spent variously in store until, with sister engines 2045/52/5/67, 32071/2, it was considered for use with Westinghouse fitted stock for the Farnborough Air Pageant in July 1950. Of the batch, all were used barring No s2060 which was found to be defective. (No 32072 was the best.) It was likely then stored at Eastbourne and probably without further use until withdrawn in November 1951. *R. C. Riley/Transport Treasury*

apparatus being removed in December 1915. This engine was subjected to cannibalism in 1935 when Eastleigh used parts from it to make a composite with the best bits from No 68, which number the 'new' engine became.

Among other experimental features foisted on the class, between 1906 and 1915 No 53 carried a Hotchkiss water circulator on the first ring of the boiler in a dome immediately abaft the chimney. This fitting was principally designed for use on stationary boilers. Precisely how well it assisted No 53 in everyday service does not appear to be in the public domain. Like all others in the class *Sirdar/Richmond* later acquired an extended smokebox.

Following his succession to the Brighton Loco Department's 'hot seat' Lawson Billinton completed Marsh's second 'J' class 4-6-2T, No 326, for which he provided Walschaerts valve gear, the first such application on the LBSCR, and Marsh's proposed order for another 10 'I3' 4-4-2Ts. These also featured several Billinton-inspired changes made largely as a result of his experience on the 'Running' side of motive power. Bogie brakes and cab clerestory roof were done away with, while Weir feed pumps superseded those driven from the crosshead. As well as the usual Westinghouse brake, vacuum brakes were installed for working 'through' traffic emanating from other companies. Sanding arrangements were also amended, particularly for effectiveness when running in reverse. In addition to all these engines he saw the last of the six Marsh

'H2' class Atlantics into traffic and the first few of his own design, the 'E2' class 0-6-0T.

In the meantime Billinton had recognised more powerful main line engines would be necessary to meet the increasing traffic demands. The most successful of these were the 'K' class 2-6-0s, so successful that despite material shortages the Government authorised the construction of five more in 1916 to bring the total in traffic to ten. (Seven of an order for ten appeared in 1921/2 but Maunsell cancelled the last three following Grouping.) He also introduced the first two of his 'L' class 4-6-4T though, as with the 'K', it was to be post-World War 1 before the final five appeared.

Lawson Billinton's final design was noted as a rebuild of his father's 'B4' though in fact so much of it was new that it is likely nothing more than the bogie and wheel centres and the splashers were taken from the original. The first 'B4X', No 55, formerly *Emperor,* emerged from Brighton Works in August 1922. Cylinders were 20in x 26in, coupled wheels 6ft 9in in diameter as in the 'B4' but set on a longer wheelbase of 10ft 0in. The boiler shell was as in the 'K' at 5ft 3in in diameter and pitched 8ft 10in above the rails. It contained 1,294.4sq ft of surface to which the Belpaire firebox, with its grate of 24.8sq ft area, contributed 139sq ft. The 21-element superheater added another 279sq ft. Pressure was 180psi, providing a tractive effort at the usual 85% of 19,645lb. Like those on the 'K', the boiler had top feed though the clacks were open rather being covered by a second dome as was commonly applied by Billinton. (Several of the 'B2X' class also received top feed boilers later but dome covered.)

The overall weight of the engine in working order was 58t 1cwt of which 37t 18cwt was adhesive. The tender, essentially that of the 'B4' but enlarged to take 3,600 gallons of water rather than the 3,000 of its progenitor, held four tons of coal and turned the scales at 39t 5cwt. The overall look of this rather handsome engine was still distinctly Billinton and distinctly Brighton too. Only one other 'B4' was 'converted' in LBSCR days, No 60 coming into traffic in September 1922. But the Southern provided another 10 between April 1923 and January 1924: these took the numbers 43/45/50/52/56/67/70-3.

The class 'nickname' was 'Greyback', the pre-Grouping 'conversions', Nos 55 and 60, having emerged from the works in grey (they never received the umber livery). But No 50, masquerading as No 52 and temporarily named *Sussex*, was also painted light grey and lined out in yellow to be photographed for Billinton in May 1923. No 50 was, incidentally, one of several of the class dual brake fitted. (No 52 had air brakes only, a means of identifying it in the photograph as an imposter.)

As befitted their new status, the class could be found working the heaviest trains on all the main lines of the LBSCR though they tended to be concentrated on the Portsmouth and Brighton routes. Even so, despite their good looks they were shown to be relatively indifferent performers when compared with other contemporary 4-4-0s drafted into the Brighton

Section – the Drummond 'L12' type for example – which took some of their former workings. During regular overhauls in the 1930s Eastleigh tinkered with them, dispensing with the feed pump and installing exhaust injectors, shifting the top feed clacks to the more customary centreline of the boiler, and exchanging Westinghouse equipment for steam brakes in five of them. They were also all brought into the Southern's composite loading gauge which essentially meant flattening the dome and the curve of the cab roof, insetting the footsteps and providing SECR-pattern 'U1' chimneys in place of Field's original. Maunsell's own design of superheater header superseded the Robinson variety as renewal became necessary. All the tenders had their coal rails sheeted.

Electrification of the Brighton line saw a number allocated to Stewarts Lane for work on the Eastern Section while several were stored in the later 1930s, only to be reinvigorated during the Dunkirk evacuation. But by that time inroads had been made into the remaining 'B4s'. All 33 engines in the class lasted long enough to receive the Southern '2000' addition to their numbers post-1931, but the first 'B4' to go was No 50, in September that year. The next out was No 65, the ex-Royal *Sandringham,* in May 1934, with No 69, the oddity *Bagshot,* following in August. The following year saw the loss of five more, including No 66 which had been renamed from *Balmoral* to *Billinton* in July 1906. Another five were gone by the end of 1936 but only one other, No 47, ex-*Canada,* was lost before the outbreak of World War 2, in July 1939.

No 2052, the former *Siemens*, dating from December 1899 (renamed *Sussex* in September 1908), another survivor into BR days. This engine was placed in store prior to World War 2 but was returned to duty at Brighton shed and worked semi-fast trains to London via the East Grinstead and Uckfield lines. A Weir feed-pump is fitted. *R. C. Riley/Transport Treasury*

The remainder of both classes reached Nationalisation, other than No 42 which succumbed in April 1947. At that time seven of the engines were at New Cross, the rest at Brighton, which sometimes saw them heading 'through' services for Bournemouth, Plymouth and South Wales, in the latter instances probably no further than Portsmouth where some of such trains would reverse. Perhaps the oddest move – albeit very temporary – was to the South Western Section to haul borrowed air-braked Eastern Region stock to/from the Farnborough Air Show on 7 and 8 August 1950. By that time the others were mostly in store, making only sporadic appearances on such traffic as Christmas mail and high-season extras.

Only Nos 2043, 2071 and 2072 received the additional BR 30000 to their numbers. But interestingly the three had different liveries: No 71 retained Bulleid 'sunshine' lettering with 'Southern' on the tender, No 43 sported lined BR black livery with 'British Railways' in full on the tender, while No 72 was the only one of the class to have fully lined BR black and the lion and wheel emblem on the tender. Twelve others unadorned and without the numerical addition were,

however, still in traffic in 1951: one of these, No 60, did carry the early 'S' prefix. But all had gone by the end of that year, the last, in December, being No 45, *Bessborough,* No 52, *Siemens/Sussex* and No 72, the 'real' *Sussex.*

It is believed that in 1904 Robert Billinton had been contemplating a 4-6-0. It would have been an interesting exercise for the observer to see what sort of improvements, if any, he made to counteract the known weaknesses in his 4-4-0s or whether it would have been like Drummond's, whose 4-6-0 types never reached, let alone exceeded, his better 4-4-0s. The addition of another driving axle was no guarantee of good riding – a rundown Stanier 'Black Five' could produce some terrible rear end antics – and continuity of the basic framing design would not address the issue of robustness. The layout of the 'B4's cylinders and valves was a step up from those of the 'B2', but would Billinton have been bold enough to look to make smoother steam passages and perhaps longer travel valves for more efficient use of steam? His son went some of the way but I somehow doubt 'Uncle Bob' would. Midland thinking was too firmly embedded.

SR No 2052 on an up train at Vauxhall, 8 July 1950. *R. C. Riley/Transport Treasury*

As BR No 32072 carrying lined black livery, this example of the 'B4X' class waits in the loading bay at Farnborough (main line) on the Saturday of the Air Pageant. Being the best of the engines selected from the class, its duty was to act as stand-by in case it was needed. The other class involved in the trains was the former LBSCR 'K' class, also air-brake fitted. *R. C. Riley/Transport Treasury.*

Bibliography

The Locomotives of the LBSCR Pts 2 and 3. D. L. Bradley, RCTS.

The London, Brighton & South Coast Railway, C. Hamilton Ellis, Ian Allan Ltd., 1960.

History of the Southern Railway, C. F. Dendy Marshall, (rev R. W. Kidner), Ian Allan Ltd., 1963.

Robert Billinton, An Engineer Under Pressure, Klaus Marx, The Oakwood Press, 2008.

Lawson Billinton, A Career Cut Short, Klaus Marx, The Oakwood Press, 2007.

Douglas Earle Marsh, His Life and Times, Klaus Marx, The Oakwood Press, 2005.

Locomotives I Have Known. J. N. Maskelyne, Percival Marshall, 1959.

The Midland Railway, C. Hamilton Ellis, Ian Allan Ltd., 4th ed. 1961.

British Railway History, 1877-1947, C. Hamilton Ellis, George Allen & Unwin, 1959.

Locomotives Illustrated, No 95, 'The Brighton 4-4-0s', Klaus Marx, RAS Publishing, 1994.

Locomotives Illustrated, No 159, 'The Locomotives built at the Southern Railway Works. 2 – Brighton, Part 1 1871-1906', W. A. T. Aves, RAS Publishing, 2005.

Locomotives Illustrated, No 84, 'The Brighton four-coupled tank engines', Klaus Marx, Ian Allan Ltd., 1992.

A number of websites have inevitably been consulted, principally for confirmatory information.

The Lost Archives of Stephen Townroe
Part 14

In this issue's selection we again have shots of the normal and the not so normal. One of the pleasures (and frustrations) of being able to access the unpublished material of SCT is the variety of situations he attended, but this is equally frustrating as sometimes we can only guess at the actual circumstances. The inclusion of views of the tablet exchange on the Lymington branch is one such example and whilst at first glance the tablet exchange problems on the S&D might appear similar, after little detective work the true circumstances come to light.

I do hope you will enjoy this penultimate selection. I know I have mentioned it before but it has been a privilege to include each selection for what is over three years now. From the correspondence I receive it seems you too enjoy it; indeed, as one reader succinctly put it a little time ago, '... the gift that keeps on giving'.

Above and overleaf: **We start this page with a view of the literal end of the line at Lymington Pier station – 'next stop Yarmouth' – if anyone ever did fail to stop; I wonder if anything ever did over-run the buffers …? There was literally enough room for an engine to run round but with pull-push operation commonplace for much of the time this was certainly not an operation that was required for every train. The ferry terminal was behind the camera and to the right the Yarmouth ferry can be seen in the channel. After this are two views of the tablet being deposited – to the arm of the signalman and also on to the collection post. Finally, we have a view of (we assume) a fireman (no name unfortunately) holding the brass tablet for the section between the Town and Pier stations and also the leather bag and metal hoop. Weighing a couple of pounds this ensemble could certainly deliver a hefty 'thwack' if not received correctly by either party; signalmen especially were known to be at risk of a broken thumb if trying to catch the hoop in the hand rather than with a closed fist, which allowed the hoop to move up the forearm more safely.**

A slight puzzler now as to the sequence. We know SCT had responsibility for SR motive power matters over the Somerset & Dorset line, indeed this route has featured previously in these instalments. Here then is a view of Highbridge with the connection across to the wharf (and the flat crossing over the GWR) via the line to the right. The former S&D Highbridge Works is also represented by the buildings to the right. What is puzzling is the sequence of the images here. Throughout this series we have been careful to incorporate the images in strict order of taking, but here we have an S&D view which is then followed by subjects non S&D related before returning again to Highbridge (and elsewhere on the S&D) later. A minor puzzle only but still intriguing.

William 'Will' H. Nicholson, Townroe's immediate boss when the latter first went to take charge at Eastleigh. Nicholson had his home at Guildford and made it plain to SCT that he had no wish to move his office to Eastleigh, thus leaving SCT with a free hand in Hampshire. The two men got on well.

A slightly unusual visitor to Eastleigh in the form of 'P' class 0-6-0 No 31325. One member of the class, usually this particular example, was at Eastleigh for many years, sometimes at Winchester City, sometimes at Southampton Docks, and even occasionally loaned to Fratton to deputise for the more usual 'Terrier' on the Hayling Island branch. Company loyalties, though, ran deep and the SECR visitor was not always welcome.

Robert and Christopher, cousins of the Townroe family, standing on the framing of an ex-works 'M7' outside the rear of Eastleigh shed.

Opposite page: 'Trains near Hinton Admiral'. A 'Lord Nelson' with a through working via the Western Region – hence the standard BR express headcode, and a Bulleid with a Bournemouth line service. (SCT does not give the loco numbers.)

Two ex-works locos, 'E1/R' No 32696, interestingly without the numerals on the smokebox plate having been picked out in white, and also 'H15' No 30491.

We now have two totally different services recorded at the lineside near Ealing (Totton). First a Bournemouth working behind a grimy 'King Arthur', No 30736 *Excalibur* working back to its home depot. The train itself is a mixture of GWR (first coach), Maunsell and then LSWR stock. After this a brace of 'M7s' with empty stock for the Fawley line, possibly on time for the evening workers' trains back to Southampton.

Above and left: We return now to Highbridge, where SCT recorded two views of the wharf, in the 1950s, no longer the hive of activity it once was. Hard to imagine that the sign seen had survived in its original position, but then what would now be referred to as collectable 'railwayana' was part of the everyday scene and it was impossible to imagine the value such items would fetch in later years.

Opposite page: A further small sequence of images relating to an incident on the S&D line where the tablet apparatus damaged a grab handle on the end of a former GWR coach working over the S&D. Respectively we see Mr Ellcot (no details but from the headgear we may assume he is an Inspector) holding a portable locomotive catcher against the miniature tablet hoop (miniature hoops were always used for remote operation although the tablet itself was of standard size) of the fixed lineside apparatus. Notice the 'paper tablet' within the hoop; this was a common test to gauge whether the lineside apparatus and locomotive equipment were correctly aligned. We then see the damage caused to the end of the GWR coach. Finally, the apparatus is attached to the tender of a Light Pacific. Engines that worked regularly over the S&D had a catcher permanently fitted whilst those that were occasional visitors ('borrowed' from Bournemouth Central depot for example) could be fitted with temporary equipment – as seen here. It appears that the temporary catcher and lineside apparatus were, for whatever reason, not aligned correctly and the receiving apparatus has become dislodged coming into contact with the lineside equipment, resulting in the former parting company with the engine and in the process damaging what was (we may assume) the first coach. We have no definite further details although the engine is No 34109, the first of the class to be trialled over the line in 1951 (the story of the trial but not the tablet incident is recounted by Peter Smith in his recent reprint *Somerset & Dorset from the Footplate*, page 53). This would also fit in with SCT's notes which record the sequence as taken in March 1951. (A further image on a similar subject appears on p91 of *SW Special No 10*.)

Above: We conclude this instalment with some views of scrapping at the rear of Eastleigh Works. To begin with locomotive scrap has been reduced to manageable 'chunks' and is loaded into open wagons. From here the journey would usually be to a steel works in South Wales. Immediately behind a Drummond 4-4-0 awaits its own fate whilst another 4-4-0 nearby is also probably not long for this world. Eastleigh South signal box on the Gosport line may also be seen in the background.

Left: This view is especially interesting as it shows the former Atlantic *Hartland Point*, Bulleid's guinea-pig for 'Leader'. With chimney and fittings removed along with the mechanical lubricators which had been sited on the framing immediately under the smokebox door, a workman may be seen on the right, no doubt in the process of effecting more stripping. Note that on one splasher at least the nameplate still remains.

Above: **Priorities! Safety glasses and gloves of course, but so it seems is the pipe, an essential element of cutting through this axle.**

Right: **More careful – in part – dismantling of 'L11' No 30134 withdrawn from Yeovil Town in early 1951. Certain parts have been more carefully removed – notice the bolts and what appears to be a clack valve on the framing; perhaps the chimney is being similarly salvaged. Again the (nowadays collectable) number plate is intact; indeed many engines from this period went for scrap with such a fitment still attached, which was subsequently destroyed with the engine.**

For our final view we have a blurred, but nevertheless interesting, view of No 36001 'decloaked' and in the process of being broken up. The bogies have already been removed and the boiler and smokebox will soon follow suit. This is No 1 end with the smokebox, boiler and firebox visible and the cab beyond.

For the final instalment in No 50: the unique Bulleid diesel shunter at Eastleigh, a derailment near Midhurst, re-roofing Bournemouth loco shed, the remains of the 'Bug', 'Mutual Improvement' competition, refuelling No 10000 at Waterloo, a 4-2-2-2 Bulleid, society wedding with a very strange liveried 'Lord Nelson', broken tyre at Itchen Abbas, and the Townroe family visiting Eastleigh carriage works.

Nostalgia at Brighton

Sean Bolan

Commensurate with the interest in Sean Bolan's images of Portsmouth (*SW48*), we are delighted to present a further small selection, this time of Brighton. (No more after this, which is a pity but the others are from 'another railway'.)

This time the views are of Brighton taken in 1947, with the exception of the concourse which is reported as 1940 (but the clock times are similar ...) and, as with Portsmouth, probably little changed for several decades. Nostalgia at its very best.

Rebuilt
The Letters and Comments Pages

We start this selection with two separate letters from Eric Youldon. (Eric, sincere apologies for the delay, hand-written notes, whilst always welcome, are sometimes left to the 'Secretary' to transcribe.)

Eric refers first to p5 of *SW43* depicting a 'T9'. Eric correctly points out the track on the right cannot be the Fawley line as the junction for this branch was beyond Totton and not at Millbrook where the image was taken. In the same issue on p40, the loco number should also be No 30804.

Eric then refers to *SW47* and the image of 'Schools' No s934 on p59. He comments, 'The date can be precisely determined. Firstly the engine is "ex-works" and fully repainted, and secondly it has been renumbered in the early short-lived BR scheme with an "S" prefix. The date therefore has to be March 1948.' (Other comments have been held over simply due to lack of space.)

On the same topic of 'those cattle wagons', Jim Smallbone called to suggest they perhaps had been empties returning to the West Country via a tortuous route. To support this, he refers us to the original *Bude Branch* book (Kingfisher) by the late David Rowe.

Next, from Pat Butler: 'As an avid follower of the *SW* I thought readers may like to see the subject that was shown on p37 of issue No 47. It is still going strong today at the Mid Hants Railway, a little modified, but you could even say the same for "S15" No 506 going past it after an 18-year overall!

'From Canute Road Crossing to the Ropley Up Inner Home signal. The photo was taken July 2019, and almost nearly in continuous use since the signal engineering department re-commissioned it from Canute Road.'

Now, from Geoffrey Pudney: 'Hello Kevin. Regarding the photograph on p63 of 'Rebuilt' in *SW46*, I recognised it straight away. I was born in and lived the first twenty odd years of my life two houses past the one in the photograph.

Above: **Another unusual image from Steve Banks which perhaps a reader can throw some light upon. This is Banbury in 1951 with a former LNER (GNR) brake attached to the rear of a through service bound for the Southern. Replacing a defective vehicle perhaps – surely not a regular diagram?**

Opposite: **The former Canute Road signal now serving as the up inner home signals at Ropley. The height of the left-hand doll has been reduced whilst lower-quadrant LSWR fittings are present. 'S15' No 506 passes with an Alresford-bound service.** *Pat Butler*

The house that can be seen is No 52 Sunnydene Road, Purley, which is a cul-de-sac off the A22 Godstone Road. There was a weekday goods train each morning down the Caterham branch which returned in the afternoon. "C2X" No 32525 was a frequent loco which provided the motive power.

'The calling-on signal was to hold the passenger service from Caterham until the Tattenham Corner service had arrived in Platform 5 at Purley station. The Caterham train would pull up behind the Tattenham Corner train and either the Caterham branch passengers would alight and walk forward and join the Tattenham Corner train or the two trains would be joined together and then go onwards to London.

'A few days ago I went to the end of Sunnydene Road and had a look at the present site. The windows of No 52 have since been "updated" and the side of the track is overgrown.

'My grandparents lived opposite our house at No 41.

Grandfather worked on the railway (SR); I think at New Cross Gate. One of his brothers and family lived next door at No 39. His other brother emigrated to USA and worked on the railroad in New York. Grandfather had an allotment on the upper side of the tracks and it can be seen in the foreground of the photograph. When quite young, during the Second World War, I recall being taken across the lines by my grandfather and helping on his allotment.

'An interesting occasion occurred later on when I was waiting on Platform 1 at Purley station for a train from Coulsdon North. There was a lot of shouting over on Platform 5 as a multiple-unit came briskly up the gradient and went straight through and out on to the main line. I later learnt that it was a driverless train which had somehow left Caterham and proceeded all the way down the branch but was (fortunately) eventually halted at Norwood Junction station.'

Gerry Nichols has recently sent us detail and illustration of an unusual working he has found whilst going through the Sid Nash photo collection in the care of the Stephenson Locomotive Society. 'I came across this photograph which was not taken by Sid but has no information as to the photographer. I believe that the photo was taken from Purley Station on 14 August 1954 when former GWR engine No 5956 *Horsley Hall* was allowed to go from Kensington Olympia to Redhill with the 07.35 Birkenhead to Margate and Ramsgate through train. Normally this train ran via Reading and Redhill but on this day an overbridge had collapsed between Guildford and Shalford Junction. There was time to divert this train via the West London line, as were the 10.40 Birmingham to Hastings, the 10.40 Birmingham to Margate and the 09.57 Wolverhampton to Margate. Richard Hardy at Stewarts Lane was hard pressed to find motive power and crews to take over from the Western Region engines, managing just two Moguls. The Stewarts Lane crew were happy to continue with the 'Hall' and it was thought that as the '43xx' Moguls were allowed, so a 'Hall' was similarly permitted. Only upon arrival at Redhill was the fact that 'Halls' were not cleared for the Brighton line evident and the engine summarily removed and sent to Redhill shed. It was eventually 'repatriated' overnight on 20 August, travelling via Earlswood to Clapham Junction, where it transferred to the Western Section Windsor Lines to access the West London Extension – subject to a speed limit of 25mph throughout and 10mph through station platforms, the obvious issue being the outside cylinder clearance.'

Now, from John King. It was through John that we received a copy of his book for review – see page 96. John, though, adds a little something else from his book which I am sure will be of interest to readers, which was not mentioned in *SW45*, nor in the biography by Klaus Marx.

Before Maunsell's successor had been decided, the SR's Indoor Assistant, W. G. Pape, took Assistant General Manager Gilbert Szlumper to lunch to meet Lawson Billinton as a possible CME successor. These are Szlumper's words from his diary – he was not impressed. 'He seems a decent sort of fellow but with an inclination towards laziness, also without polish. I would not fancy him as Locomotive Engineer somehow'. In the event, Szlumper was to play an important role in the SR board's selection of Bulleid.

During the 1939-45 conflict, Lawson Billinton was for a period working for the War Office under Lt-Col Manton, the Commandant No 2, Railway Training Centre, Derby (the former LMS School of Transportation), although perhaps surprisingly Klaus Marx did not mention this in his biography of him. Exactly what he was doing has not been discovered but again Szlumper makes negative comments in his diary. Szlumper was ostensibly still General Manager (he had succeeded Walker in 1937) but he had been seconded to the War Office as Director-General of Transportation & Movements. It was on 5 January 1940 (after a visit to Derby) that Szlumper recorded in his diary that Manton had had to get rid of Lawson Billinton as he had grown very lazy and unimaginative. 'He can only think of somewhat old-fashioned main line steam loco practice and when asked to produce a training scheme for military railway purposes, was only able after a long interval to put about three-quarters of a sheet of paper with no tangible suggestions. I told Manton that if Billinton had been any use, he would have been on the Southern after amalgamation in 1923.'

Now a delighted piece of nostalgia from Graham Buxton-Smither on the subject of commuting and 'one-upmanship'. 'A favourite involved me in some cheating on a crossword. This had all came about as I had to endure a fellow commuter every morning who used to do the *Guardian* crossword amid loud self-congratulatory outbursts when he solved a clue; it used to annoy me and the other passengers but he persisted. I too was a devotee of that paper's compilers (especially the fiendish Auracaria who often bested me) but I rarely tried the crosswords on the journey. Anyhow, I got so fed up with this after a few months that I decided to shame him into submission so I spent a late evening in London and caught one of the last two trains

We have recently been privileged to access the colour slides and black and white photographs of the late Graham Smith. At the time of writing the task of scanning is being undertaken but some gems have already appeared like this view of 4Sub S5210 at Sidcup on a typical suburban service in March 1953.

to Windsor at Waterloo. This meant I was able to buy an early edition of the next day's papers, duly bought the Guardian and started on the cryptic crossword. Just for once the brain was firing on all cylinders and by the time I got off at Windsor & Eton Riverside Station and strolled up to my apartment next to the castle, it was complete. So, 07:45 came around and I was waiting on the platform for the train to disgorge its few passengers before taking my accustomed window seat opposite our nemesis and, unusually, I struck up a conversation with 'Crossword Christopher' once we were fully boarded and on our way to Datchet: "I see it's Auracaria today," as we both surveyed the puzzle page; "I've not tried a cryptic crossword before, is it as challenging as you make it sound?" "Oh yes," he replied. "Especially this one – I always finish him but not usually on a single journey." I asked him to wish me luck and got down to it. His usual triumphal noises confirmed that he had solved two clues as we approached Sunnymeads; another as we neared Wraysbury. Just before we got to Staines, I "completed" my crossword – and, showing him the page, saying "I thought you said this was a tough one; I don't think I'll bother in future." To cut a long story short, he changed carriages after that and never bothered us again. It also pays to know your stations as I'd often watched bundles of newspapers being carried into Waterloo late at night and so spotted the newspaper seller offering the first editions from about 11pm onwards.'

I must now sit corrected, as at least three readers have advised me of the following. I will use Roger MacDonald's letter as the example. 'Thank you for publishing the splendid colour interlude feature in *SW47*, but I think the caption to the illustration at the bottom of page 35 is incorrect. The location is not St Denys but rather the train headed by *Exmouth* is leaving Poole station in the Up direction. The engine headcode displayed is for passenger trains between Bournemouth Central and Weymouth. In the background Poole station can just be seen and the train has already gone over one level crossing and is now about to pass over the High Street level crossing controlled by Poole "A" signal box. The shot was taken from the adjacent footbridge provided for pedestrians when the gates were closed. Bearing the date 1872, it is still in existence and used, and many was the occasion when, as a nipper in the 1950s, I stood on it and watched "T9s", "M7s" and the like pass beneath me ...'

We move on now to Stephen Duffell's piece on the fatalities in Wallers Ash (*SW47*) with some additional comments by Peter Clarke: 'I am writing to add a couple of observations on Stephen Duffell's article on the Wallers Ash accident in 1842 (*SW47* p6). Firstly I was interested to read that the surgeon who gave evidence at the inquest was Mr. H. Lyford. This would have been Mr Henry Giles Lyford who was a member of a distinguished family of surgeons who had served the

Below and opposite page: **Something we have been intending to include for some time are the few views of the CL24 diesel-electric locomotives while they were working on the Eastern section of the Southern Region. Seventeen of the class, Nos D5000-14 and D5016-18, were allocated to the South Eastern lines between January 1959 and April 1960, all being based at Hither Green. This was to cover for delays in the delivery of stock for the first phase of the Kent Coast electrification. But there was a problem, as the CCE considered them too heavy for use and to rectify this the complete batch had to have their train-heat boilers temporarily removed. Later some were retro fitted and might be seen working in tandem with a 'D65xx' locomotive, which type was only equipped with electric train heating. All returned to the LMR between May 1960 and November 1962. Seen here are Nos D5002/11/14, proving they might work a variety of services, from passenger at an unreported location (the single disc would indicate a Mid-Kent line train) to a down coal train at Martin Mill in July 1962. Seen standing idle is D5011 in Gillingham in March 1960.** *All Arthur Taylor*

Hampshire County Hospital continuously since 1768. His father had been Jane Austen's doctor after she moved to Winchester in 1817 and he subsequently served three terms of office as Mayor of the city.

'At the time of the accident, the hospital was in Parchment Street, Winchester. The hospital was used to dealing with railway related accidents as it had treated navvies injured while building the line between Basingstoke and Winchester between 1838 and 1840. The line passed through the estate of the wealthy and influential landowner Sir Thomas Baring, who had been the first chairman of the London & South Western Railway (then called the London & Southampton Railway). Sir Thomas took a great interest in the affairs of the hospital and managed to persuade the board of the L&SWR to make a donation of £100 to hospital funds (about £10,000 in today's money).

'The accident at Wallers Ash goes to illustrate how hazardous working on the railways was in those early days. The pressure on the infirmary from railway-related and other accidents and the incidence of disease meant that the hospital was chronically short of space for patients and it was not until 1868 that it was able to move from Parchment Street to its present location on the Romsey Road.

'It is sad to record that the line between Worting Junction and Wallers Ash has been prone to several railway accidents (and suicides) over the years including:

• A derailment in Wallers Ash cutting of the 10 o'clock train from Nine Elms less than a fortnight after the line was opened throughout from London to Southampton in May 1840, killing the driver and stoker and injuring some passengers;

• The collapse of Wallers Ash tunnel in 1842 in which four labourers were killed and seven injured and the subsequent incident which involved the derailment of an Up luggage train (covered comprehensively by Stephen's article);

• A fatal accident in 1911 in which the senior porter at Micheldever station, William Strode, was killed while crossing the tracks;

• A fire in 1936 on a Channel Islands boat train from Southampton Docks while passing through Micheldever which, thankfully, only resulted in eight minor injuries;

• Two derailments on the Up relief line at the Weston Colley loop, the first in 1946 involving a freight train hauled by Class S15 locomotive No 502, and the second in 1986 involving another freight train hauled by Class 33 diesel locomotive then numbered D6535;

• An oil spillage at the oil terminal at Micheldever in 1983;

• A collision in the cutting between the two Popham tunnels in 1985 in which a Class 33 diesel locomotive ran into a stranded EMU which had been immobilised by a chalk slip on the Up line. The locomotive had been sent to rescue the EMU. The most serious injury was to the driver of the locomotive who was trapped in his cab, whilst his assistant and 11 passengers on the EMU

suffered various degrees of personal injury. It was miraculous that there were no fatalities given the extent of the damage to the locomotive cab and the EMU;

• Another collision in Litchfield tunnel in 1986 in which a Class 47 light locomotive ran into the back of a stationary ballast train during an engineer's possession. The driver of the locomotive was killed but the driver's assistant escaped with minor injuries;

• And finally, a fire in the engine room of a Class 70 locomotive at Micheldever in April 2012.

'Hopefully, with modern signalling systems and improved safety procedures accidents such as these will now be a thing of the past.'

Now, from Brian Kidman on the subject of the Croydon, Oxted & East Grinstead Railway. 'Dear Kevin. I was on the point of writing to ask if we might be treated to more of those wonderful sepia prints of Croydon, Oxted & East Grinstead Railway structures, as featured and promised in a couple of much earlier issues of *SW*, when I picked up *SW46* and, lo and behold, there they were, together with an excellent article by Jeremy Clarke. I was particularly pleased to find the view of Oxted Viaduct in as-built condition – which I shall attempt to reproduce in model form, when time permits. I'd hoped that a plan of the structure might have survived, but my enquiries with Network Rail contacts drew a blank. Having conducted a photographic survey and produced plans already, it was apparent that the structure had been altered over the years, but I now know how it would have looked originally, so thank-you! Incidentally, when it was built I believe it was known as Limpsfield Viaduct, Limpsfield being the predominant parish at that time.

'As regards Oxted Station, the down bay platform line has now been electrified – I'm not sure when, but quite recently. And, earlier this year, the enormous and long disused 1960s gasholder that dominated the town and station, has finally been dismantled and removed to make way for a residential development. I have a 1:2500 scale OS map, dated 1935, which shows two smaller gasholders on the site, one or both of which may have been original. In addition to the area of control Jeremy mentions, the new Oxted signal box must be contacted to authorise movements on and off the Bluebell Line connection at East Grinstead. This was a regular occurrence for the "Waste by Rail" spoil removal trains, and occasionally since for rail charters, visiting locomotives and transfers of stock, including Bluebell's main-line certified 100-plus-year-old Metropolitan Railway carriages, hired by London Underground for their Steam on the Met programmes.

'Following closure of the Woodside Line, egress from the Anglo-American siding at Selsdon onto the Oxted Line was controlled by a ground shunt signal. The junction was replaced with plain line some time after the siding ceased to be used, although the shunt signal remained in-situ, displaying a red aspect, for a further 10 years or so!

'I worked in London and was a regular commuter on the Oxted Line between 1979 and 2006. Electrification in 1987

The man in the centre should need no introduction to readers of *SW* – but, just in case, it is no other than Dr Richard Beeching, Chairman of British Railways from 1963 until 1965 but whose legacy is still spoken of today. He is seen on the platform at Three Bridges – the other individuals are not mentioned but it must be said the man on Beeching's left bears a striking resemblance to Gerry Fiennes. Beeching is blamed for almost every railway closure regardless of the decade in which it occurred and we should remember he not only closed lines but also intermediate stations on routes which remained open, as well as various workshops. Whether he was right or wrong, both generally and in specific cases, will continue to be debated for as long as railways exist, but it should be remembered he was simply the figurehead: the cuts had in the main been proposed by the managers on the actual regions, although these shadowy figures remained hidden and nowadays are mostly forgotten more than half a century later. *Paul Cooper*

brought about a huge improvement in service reliability, but I still fondly remember the DEMUs, with their idiosyncracies, unpredictability and occasional incidents. One of the evening treats was seeing how fast drivers could propel their charges on the downhill run through Oxted tunnel anticipating when they would have to make a brake application on the dash towards Oxted. Following the usual commuter custom, this caused little anxiety and heads would continue to be buried behind newspapers. On one summer evening, however, the anticipated brake application didn't occur. After a few seconds, newspapers were lowered and anxious glances exchanged between fellow travellers. Finally, there was a very heavy brake application, but far too late. We sailed through Oxted station and on over the viaduct, finally coming to a stand well inside Limpsfield Tunnel. Anxious glances continued to be exchanged until, after five minutes or so, we very slowly reversed back into the station. The subject of a "please explain" no doubt! On another hot summer evening, a burning smell began to percolate our carriage as we ran through Selhurst station. Newspapers were lowered and, as we drew to a stand at East

Croydon's Platform 6, smoke started to drift around our carriage. Perhaps surprisingly, no-one moved except for a few alighting passengers, until the guard came on the PA to announce, very calmly, "good evening ladies and gentlemen. I regret to inform you that this train will be terminating here, as it is on fire. All change please." I avoided travelling in the DEMU motor coaches if at all possible, due to their hard suspension and ability, when climbing under load, to provide one with an at-seat all-body massage, usually from the inside out!

'Peak-hour business trains to/from London Bridge provided variety and entertainment. Almost invariably hauled by Class 33 diesel locomotives, these seriously struggled on the morning climb up through Oxted Tunnel, the slow crawl meaning that the coach dynamos were inoperative and we would progress in faintest candlelight. An additional issue was the propensity of County School students to switch off the lights from the control boxes situated at the end of the Mk1 coaches, before they jumped out at Oxted station. Always worth checking before the tunnel was reached! Very rarely, a Class 47 loco would deputise. Good news, since it guaranteed

Our friend Roger Simmonds has a habit of picking up images from decades past and here are two more he has recently sourced. The first depicts a waiting porter at Ryde and the second, which personally I think the more interesting, shows a train entering Whitwell station from Ventnor West. There are no dates for either although the Whitwell image must be prior to 1926 when the passing loop – the only one between Merstone and Ventnor West – was taken out of use.

a rapid ascent through the tunnel and adequate lighting. One morning a Class 47 appeared hauling a Western Region coach set, complete with micro-buffet, though, sadly, unmanned.

'I recall also incidents following electrification of the Oxted Line. On one evening our train was terminated at East Croydon due to a traction-power supply failure. As successive East Grinstead-bound trains arrived from London Bridge and Victoria, Platforms 5 and 6 became ever more packed and tensions mounted. Eventually, an East Grinstead train was announced from one of the other platforms, causing a sudden surge of people through the narrow subway. We were astonished to see a raspberry-ripple-liveried Class 73 and air-conditioned Gatwick Express set arrive which, we were assured, was going to East Grinstead, first stop Oxted. Some persuasion was necessary before people started to board, but run to East Grinstead it most certainly did!'

Next, it is Mike King's turn with some notes on *SW47* with reference to 'Slip Coaches' and 'Salisbury-Exeter'.

'Thoroughly enjoyed the latest issue. A few points, if I may: Set 696 at Margate. The "Continental" brake third visible is coach

3589, formerly one end of set 900 – this set number is just visible in the dirt above 696 and was an excursion/special traffic set based on the South Eastern section from 1957-59; so probably saw duty for just a few days each year. The coach interior pictured is a Southern-designed (Maunsell/Lynes) unclassed open saloon and not one of SECR origin – the SECR 1921-27 boat train coaches were all side corridor vehicles with the occasional first class saloon in the brake end coaches, but set 696 did indeed include several of the SR vehicles in the formation – one is just visible behind coach 3589.

'Jeffery Grayer's article on the Salisbury-Exeter did bring back memories as I witnessed the decline of the service from the viewpoints of Waterloo, Surbiton and Woking. However, the demise of some of the Bulleid Pacifics seems to have been missed from the table on page 81 (a proofing problem, I would guess, as they are in a batch?). Those missing are:

34075 Allocation ended 4/64
34076 Allocation ended 9/64
34078 Allocation ended 9/64
34079 Allocation ended 9/64
34080 Allocation ended 9/64
34081 Allocation ended 8/64
34083 Allocation ended 8/64
34084 Allocation ended 11/63
34086 Allocation ended 9/64

'Of these, 34076/79/84/86 moved east along with some of the others listed by Jeffery, the others departed to South Wales scrapyards in due course. A visit to Exeter and Exmouth Junction in late July 1964 found No 34075 stored at the old GWR shed at St David's, No 34083 on the Exmouth Junction scrapline in company with a couple of Moguls, while Nos 34062/70 were stored in the sidings to the south of the line at 72A – not to run again - the others still allocated to "the Junction" at that time were all still in use.

'On that day the 07.30 up from Exeter was passed outside Salisbury hauled by No D810 *Cockade*. My first sighting of a "Warship" on the route was on the same train at Surbiton a few weeks earlier, with No D815 *Druid*. I took a photo, but eventually was so disgusted with the replacement diesel locos that I binned the print!! Eventually, all the Swindon-built "Warships" were noted, including the pilot prototypes D800-802, but never was a North British-built loco seen. "Hymeks" appeared occasionally on Sundays, including the one remaining Sunday down milk empties, which passed Surbiton at about 5.05pm. The former 4pm Clapham Junction-Exeter milk empties, on which I had "copped" so many Exmouth Junction Pacifics at about 4.20pm (weekday timings), had ceased to run from 6 September 1964, being routed instead via the WR main line – presumably as a prelude to singling which reduced line capacity considerably. Presumably, this was not an issue on a Sunday evening. Despite seeing the "milks" regularly in 1963/64, some Pacifics never appeared – these being 34020/30/75/78/83 – much to the disappointment of the Surbiton Grammar School band of spotters who gathered

A slightly unusual perspective on a Bulleid. No clue as to the identity but as this was 1957 it is likely to be a rebuilt 'Merchant Navy'.

by the railway cutting outside the school before and after lessons. Such were our numbers, that the school prefects were in the habit of blowing the whistle to "fall-in" for assembly on that side of the playground to remove the excuse that we did not hear it!! Many a time was I almost marked late in the register for hanging on to see the next steam service. Those were the days … Also, the Mogul seen at Yeovil cannot be No 31822, as this was the prototype "N1", so I suggest it is "U" class 31802 which was a Yeovil engine in 1963/64.

'Finally, No 34041 disabled after the Woking accident of 23/12/55 is berthed in Oatlands sidings, between Weybridge and Walton-on-Thames – presumably the nearest location that the train could access following the incident. The electric unit involved was 4-COR 3147, the rear motor coach being S11212S, which was repaired subsequently using the second-hand underframe of similar motor coach No 11082, whose body had been destroyed by a flying bomb at Wimbledon as long ago as 29 June 1944. The underframe had been stored since then – clearly someone knew it might come in useful. The Southern knew all about recycling long before it became fashionable.'

Lastly for this issue, from Mike Burgess, and again on the subject of 'Slip Coaches' from *SW47*: 'I found David Austin's article on this subject quite fascinating, and whilst reading the section on accidents and mishaps, something triggered a recollection I had of reading an accident report of an incident involving slip coaches at Tonbridge. Some years ago, I did some research on the Tonbridge to Redhill line, and discovered an online copy of the Board of Trade accident report, which at the time I summarised as follows:

"Tonbridge, 30 September 1866. This accident occurred in the last years prior to the opening of the Sevenoaks cut off. The 7.25am mail train from London to Dover included a portion at the rear which on Sundays was slipped from the train as it ran through Tonbridge station to provide a service from Tonbridge to Hastings. On this particular Sunday, the train consisted of twelve carriages of which the first eight were bound for Dover and Deal, and the remaining four were to form the Hastings service. The train was running late due to fog, and was approaching Tonbridge from Penshurst at about 50mph. The guard responsible for carrying out the slip was in the first coach of the Hastings portion. He detached the coupling on the falling

Happy in your work …? Passengers alighting from an Effingham Junction service at Waterloo, circa 1980.

gradient approaching Tonbridge and applied the brake, but due to weather conditions the wheels slipped on the rails and the carriages were running too fast on the approach to the station. The practice was for the main train to pass the station on the through line and after it had cleared the loop points, the signalman would change them to bring the slip portion into the down platform. On this occasion, the slip portion was travelling at about 30mph and it failed to stop in the platform, running through the station before hitting an empty train of seven carriages 262 yards beyond the station. Eleven passengers and the guard were injured but there were no fatalities."

'The inspector (Lieutenant Colonel F. W. Rich) objected to the practice of slipping coaches which he considered to be dangerous, and in this case also objected to the practice of changing the points between the two portions of the train, as this required the speeding train to run over unlocked facing points (always considered to be an unsafe practice on passenger lines). The use of slip coaches before the days of

vacuum or air brakes may have offered some convenience to the railway companies but must have been hazardous when sole reliance was placed on the guard's handbrake.

'The report clearly bears out the misgivings that the inspector had in relation to the practice of slipping coaches, particularly in this instance the inexperience of the guard who had only previously slipped coaches on three previous occasions (all at Caterham); and to the practice of changing the points to allow the slipped coaches into the down platform loop. The full report can be found on the www.railwaysarchive.co.uk website. Of course, this accident predates the fitting of continuous brakes, and requirements of the 1889 legislation requiring the interlocking of points and signals, but it does suggest that the practice in the early days was not exactly free from hazards.'

From the Transport Treasury Archive

We have recently accessed some of the amazing photographs at The Transport Treasury. I deliberately say 'some', as the collection runs to in excess of 500,000 views, not all Southern of course, and I think even I would end up with square eyes were it possible to view them all.

Looking at a list of images will reflect the content but as the original photographer may have had his own specific method of recording material, the crucial points would possibly be known only to him. Whatever, the images themselves deserve far better than being confined to negative packets, so again in another regular series we will be depicting examples from the archive and attempting to show examples from the work of several collections, both name and subject related.

We start with Alec Swain, a professional railwayman who was also the one-time Shedmaster at Willesden. One of his particular attributes was that he never took a photograph unless the weather and conditions were to his particular liking.

We start with three works images. The Swain list is not always helpful in identifying specific dates and locations but we are pretty certain the first view is the interior of Brighton and then we have two of Eastleigh. The Brighton image is almost as much a view of dismantling as it is of repair with (on the left) 'D' No 31574, 'M7' No 30039 and two LMS Fairburn design 2-6-4Ts, the lead being No 42074. Behind the second Fairburn could be a 'R1' tank. On the right is another 'M7', No 30322. The clutter on the ground is extraordinary, trip hazards at the very least – we assume the works knew what it was doing. There is no date unfortunately but from the lack of activity perhaps it is a Sunday? On the extreme right the name 'Peating' appears on the sack barrow – probably the name of the Foreman in that particular shop. *Alec Swain/Transport Treasury*

Sunday morning at Eastleigh perhaps – can we also say this has a slightly better appearance with a fair attempt made to keep the marked walkways clear? A good number of the Western Section Southern types are also represented, from a 'USA', a 'Q' perhaps behind, Bulleid Pacifics, a 'Lord Nelson' and a Urie 4-6-0. In the first view the Bulleid in the centre distance is probably a 'Merchant Navy': even without specific number/name identification the original 'Merchant Navies' always appeared 'fatter' when viewed head-on. The second view shows an 'O2' and No 34048 – just look also at that asbestos lagging around the dome of the 'O2'.

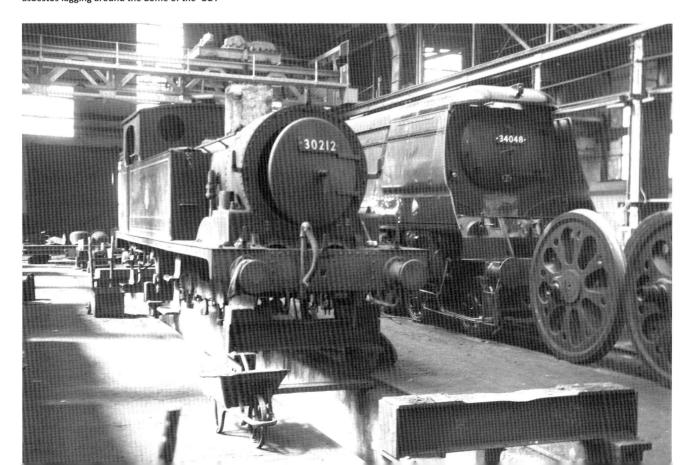

One locomotive we can identify is this 'C2X', No 32544. Built in 1911, the engine had a 50-year life, with its final decade spent at Norwood Junction, where this photograph was taken on 3 October 1952. Behind it are two Bulleid 'Q' class locomotives (the first 30537, the second not identified). To the left is 'E4X' 0-6-2T No 32466.

Rear end view of 'C' No 1582 at Stewarts Lane: tender coupling correctly stowed and likewise the vacuum pipe. The notice on the right warns against the disposal of ashes in this particular area. Is the pipe reaching cross the tender a spray for damping down the coal after fuelling?

We move sheds this time to Nine Elms where 'U' No 1611 waits outside the shed, again with correct stowage of the coupling at least. If you look carefully a member of the crew can seen on the loco framing, cleaning the lookout glasses at the front of the cab perhaps? Loco crew, firemen especially, were expected to be agile, with limited handrails and often slippery footholds an accepted risk. It would take the coming of Mr Bulleid to consider this essential aspect of footplate work with the provision of tubular ladders on the rear of the tender. In the background a 'Lord Nelson' is arriving after running light from Waterloo.

This is a view rarely photographed, showing part of the turntable mechanism at Nine Elms. No details are given although from the image we can clearly see the engine being turned is a 'Paddlebox'. The turntable seen was replaced in later years, removing the side girders.

Loco detail in the form of a Weir pump and Westinghouse pump. The specific engine is not identified but may well be an Ashford 'C'.

'N15X' No (3)2339 *Stephenson* minus at least its centre set of driving wheels. The usual reason for such work was to attend to an axle box defect and whilst in certain cases the actual set of wheels may of necessity have to be returned to a main works, the actual lifting and removal of the axle set was undertaken at the sheds. No details given as to date or location.

Finally in this section we have a view of the Stewarts Lane breakdown crane and match truck, of Cowans Sheldon manufacture and rated at 15 tons. The crane would be continuously kept in light steam and so ready for any contingency although with ever heavier locomotives and rolling stock its use must have been limited. Even so it lasted until 1963.

Kangaroos and Keys at Knowl

Amyas Crump

The definitive holiday image: Sidmouth. *Amyas Crump collection*

There can be little doubt that Bulleid locomotive designs raised eyebrows across the Southern at the end of World War 2 and on in to the British Railways era. To this day one of the most conservative corners of the Southern system must be Sidmouth (No 34010) and yet the town provides an insight into SR thinking and planning, every bit as eyebrow raising as an air-smoothed Pacific.

Even in the early 1800s, Sidmouth was a growing and thriving town (also putting to work the first steam locomotive west of Radstock, but that is probably not a story for *SW*!). One part of that expansion was the building of a rather rustic structure with the name 'Knowl Cottage' (later sources tend to use the spelling 'Knowle' – as per the former hospital and railway halt in Hampshire). By c1820 this property had come into the ownership of one Thomas Fish (whose immense and recently acquired wealth included 400 public houses). After some alteration, it was Fish who first opened his property to the public, as an attraction – with free admission on Mondays.

Quite extraordinarily, and beside the wealth of cultural and artistic exhibits indoors, the grounds (whose acreage has varied greatly through different owners) contained six kangaroos, fifty parrots, two buffalo, a camel, a pelican, an emu and antelopes. By comparison, London Zoo opened eight years later in 1828. No wonder tourists came from far and wide – with no more than 30 to be admitted, every 15 minutes – hence little wonder that thoughts turned to the building of a railway. The menagerie and curios remained popular attractions for some 40 years before the estate was broken up and sold off. By way of illustration of the wealth associated with the house in Victorian times, furniture from there is now in the collection of the V&A. When the railway finally came to Sidmouth in 1874, it was the nearby grounds of the Knowl where much of the festivities were undertaken.

The year 1882 brought further change, with Knowl much enlarged and now in much reduced grounds, becoming a hotel. Regarded as having the most beautiful hotel gardens in Devon, the years up to World War 2 were good. Interestingly, the hotel did not appear to advertise in the GWR's famous

'M7' No 30024 with the branch train at the terminus shortly to depart for Tipton St Johns and Sidmouth Junction. *Amyas Crump collection*

Holiday Haunts, unlike most of Sidmouth's other important hotels, the Westcliff even offering to send a car 16 miles to meet trains at Exeter St Davids! Knowl, however, settled for a horse-drawn bus meeting just the local branch trains.

In common with many large hotels it was requisitioned by the military, becoming RAF Sidmouth and also the victim of a German 'tip and run' raid, finally returning to civilian use on 1 May 1947, at which time it boasted 60 bedrooms.

With nationalisation so clearly on the horizon, how was it that, in October 1947, the local *Sidmouth Observer* announced that the Southern Railway had acquired the hotel? At this time John Elliot (later Sir John Elliot) was Acting SR General Manager, and although there is no directly relevant information within his autobiography (*On and Off the Rails*,

Allen & Unwin 1982), there is reference to a clear policy of 'best foot forward' and 'go down with all flags flying' (p65) at the end of independence and the absorption of the Southern into the newly nationalised network.

As with the other former railway owned hotels, Knowl became part of the BTC Hotels group, whilst clearly it was the railway connection that brought the 'Anglo-French Railway Conference' to the place in November 1948, attended by amongst others the same John Elliot. Railway ownership was to be brief, for despite apparent commercial success, it was sold off in summer 1951. As early as 1952 it was scheduled by the Ministry of Housing and Local Government, as being of outstanding historical and architectural interest, with all the grounds covered by a tree preservation order.

The former Knowle House/Hotel and grounds. *Amyas Crump collection*

Faded glory: part of the former ballroom. *Amyas Crump collection*

Sadly, as with so very many historic buildings, that was not to mean much. The hotel closed its doors on 28 September 1968, followed shortly after by an auction sale of the contents. It was sold to the local Urban District Council – for conversion to social housing flats and council offices. Further change came through changes in local government, with an expansion of the office accommodation – partly in a new wing.

To the great dismay of many, that new wing became part of the reason for the waiving of the outstanding status of the building and permission was given for it to be demolished with flats to be built on the site – the council also moving to new offices.

It was boarded up and empty, pending its bat population being rehoused, when I was fortunate in being able to have a quick look around just as the last of the contents were being cleared. There was still clear evidence of many of the stages of Knowl's history but there remained one real challenge – to locate something from its limited time in Southern ownership. And there it was: inspired by that shade of green paint on a cupboard door, here was something truly tangible. Small perhaps but nevertheless unmistakably Southern – a humble key!

Right: **Paintwork from a loose plank within a cleaner's cupboard – Southern green ...?** *Amyas Crump collection*

Below right: **A key could be from anywhere but there is no doubting the origins of this ash tray – if proof were required, it has been engraved to deter the souvenir hunter ...** *Amyas Crump collection*

The

KNOWLE HOTEL

A.A.   R.A.C.

One of the most distinguished Hotels in the Country

8 acres of beautiful gardens	Excellent, and varied, cuisine
3 spacious lounges facing	Fully licensed. Well equip-
South and overlooking the sea	ped garage with private lock-
Private suites available	ups in the Hotel grounds

SPECIAL TERMS FOR RESIDENTS

For Terms apply to the Resident Manager
Knowle Hotel, Sidmouth, South Devon

Telephone : Sidmouth 5   Telegrams : Knowle, Sidmouth

35

The Bulleid Graveyard
Images from the Wilf Stanley Collection
at The Transport Treasury

It is a fact of life that today's latest produce will be tomorrow's cast off, railways, their locomotives, units, and rolling stock, no exception. Specifically, so far as the steam locomotive is concerned, new – cascade – scrap had been the common feature for over 130 years, that is until the final decade of steam working when the 'cascade' word ceased to apply and apart from the few engines rescued for preservation the vast majority ended up being scrapped – 'recycled' might be a better word more appropriate to the language of today.

Above and spread overleaf: **Engines would arrive at the breakers relatively intact – or at least with the tender coupled. Coupling rods were usually either in the tender or poked through the firebox doors. The weight of these combined might perhaps be the equivalent of a ton or so and the breakers would certainly complain if such parts were missing. Examples of both the 'Merchant Navy' and Light Pacific types are visible, with some still having glass in the cab windows, although it will be noted on the engine alongside No 35008 that the cab fittings are already missing. Because of their value such pieces were removed the moment the engine arrived.**

Apart from stripping the cab of non-ferrous metals the next thing to go was the tender. Several Bulleid tenders were sold to the South Wales steel mills where – minus the tender tank of course – they were used as ingot carriers.

It appears the next stage was to strip the actual boiler of its contents, namely the tubes. Images of the dismantling appear to show a different order applied to different engines but this could very well have been simply down to the preference of the various scrapping gangs.

So far as the Southern Region was concerned, we can appreciate why after 50 years' service a Drummond 4-4-0 might well come to the end of its days; less easy to understand the wholesale cull of the Brighton 'K' class at the end of 1962, and even more difficult to comprehend the setting aside of comparatively modern steam engines, namely the Bulleid rebuilds after a life counted in single figure years. But then when Mr Jarvis and co worked their magic there was no comprehension of the speed modernisation would take; steam was yesterday's friend, today it was outmoded, outdated and unwanted, and setting aside the romantic ideal associated with steam, we should not forget working with steam seven days a week in conditions that had changed little in the past 100 years was hardly something likely to attract a new generation of footplate staff.

Here Nos 35023 and 35008 are not long for this world; certainly the remains of the former are already beyond the miracles the preservationists have achieved in recent times.

An engine minus identity: about the only neatness in the whole scene is the way the tubes and elements have been sorted.

A new, albeit very temporary, wheel arrangement for these Bulleids.

The Southern Way

Issue 49

Consequently, it was really not much of a surprise to see steam disappear as quickly as it did. In the final few years the various locomotive works where engines had once quietly gone to be dismantled ('dismantled' somehow seems a kinder word compared with the harshness of the term 'scrapping') were unable to cope with the influx of withdrawn engines and recourse had to be made to outside yards and contractors.

The only located view of an original Pacific in the yard, but again dealt with in the same way.

And towards the end, just so much steel plate. Many of the pieces in the foreground seemingly originated from a Bulleid type, perhaps even the former No 35007.

No more pristine external condition after overhaul, no more slipping out of Waterloo bound for Exeter or Bournemouth. No more preparation on a wet winter's evening for a crew, or last-minute servicing. Yesterday's technology being recycled into … whatever.

We will not dwell further on what happened leading up to July 1967 – that is well known, and what is also known is that those machines that managed to soldier on to the end almost entirely ended up in South Wales at sites where, unlike at Messrs Woodhams, dismantling, perhaps 'dismembering' would be more accurate, took place and these sad scenes were recorded during 1968.

And finally a tender that did not find a further use.

Farewell to Steam 'Over the Alps' 1966 (A Trilogy of Railtours) Part 1

'The S15 Commemorative Railtours' Organised by the Locomotive Club of Great Britain

Les Price

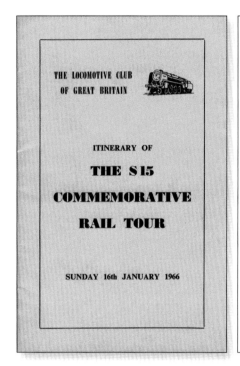

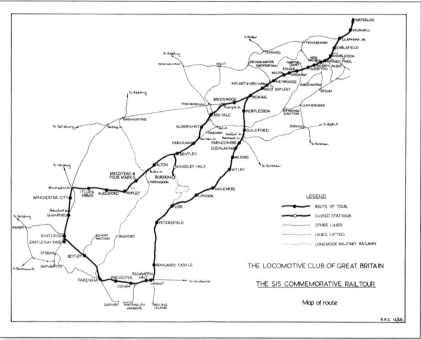

During the final years of steam, there were five 'Specials' which crossed 'The Alps' between Alton and Winchester Junction between January and March 1966. These were the last such trains over the section, and I was fortunate to be able to travel on three of them.

The first was the 'S15 Commemorative Rail Tour'. Due to popular demand this train ran in two parts, the first on Sunday 9 January and the second on the following Sunday. My brother and I were on the second.

The first was booked for six coaches but due to the demand was loaded to seven, according to Tony Deller, shedmaster at Feltham at the time; this was one vehicle over what was officially permitted. Five days before the tour, the chosen 'S15' was taken on a test run, leaving Feltham shed around 11am and getting back at 2pm. This was because by then it had been out of service for over five months.

Despite the additional load, the 'S15' stormed the 1 in 60 three-mile climb from Butts Junction to Medstead, losing just one minute on the twelve-minute schedule from Alton, a very creditable effort. In the event, this tour ran pretty much to time throughout, apart, that is, for an eight-minute delay waiting at Winchester Junction, probably due to late running on the mainline.

The following Sunday's train was loaded to eight coaches, which taking account of Tony Deller's above remark, was now two over regulation. Notwithstanding the previous week's performance, this time the engine was given assistance on the climb for this Rail Tour.

The itinerary and map for the second 'S15' commemorative tour.

The first tour (which had sold out) hauled by 'S15' No 30837 storming past Woking. The image was taken by Michael Foster from the footplate of 'N' class No 31403, one of three engines coupled together waiting for a road back to Guildford. Two of the three had been on overnight engineering works trains and the third from a regular night freight duty.

The same 9 January tour, this time leaving Alresford. *Roger Thornton*

At Bentley, No 30837 has come to a stand whilst No 31639 waits – masked in steam – on the up line. *Les Price*

Dealing specially with the trip of 16 January, this started from Waterloo where the platforms were dusted with snow, perhaps an appropriate prequel to a trip 'over the Alps'. Promptly at 9.15am No 30837 was away and ran virtually to schedule to Bentley where the covering of snow added a little drama; it was cold and bleak. Our pilot was due to join us here, 'U' class 2-6-0 No 31639 manned by a Guilford crew which was waiting for us on the 'Up' line.

First, though, the 'U' changed places with the 'S15', the latter coming off the train and No 31639 taking us for the short run down the branch to Bordon, and its long association with military traffic. Originally the Bordon Light Railway, the line was contemporary with the Woolmer Instructional Military Railway (later the Longmoor Military Railway).

The Bordon branch line opened on 11 December 1905, but the military line connected to it did not finally reach Liss until the early 1930s. The passenger service on the Borden branch was withdrawn on 16 September 1957 and the line closed completely less than three months after the visit of the railtour on 4 April 1966. It is likely that our tour that day may well have been the last time passengers travelled on the branch.

The crew of No 31639 on 16 January 1966, photographed at Bordon. Fireman Mick Foster is on the left and with him Driver Sid Woods. Standing in front is a very dapper retired Reading Southern Guard, Ray Ruffell, who both crew knew well. The photograph was taken by Ray's wife. *Michael Foster collection*

Opposite page: No 31639 arriving at and in the process of running round at Bordon. Already the fixed signalling has been removed and it is likely a railwayman was present to 'clip and padlock' the requisite turnouts to permit passenger working. *Roger Thornton*

Back at Bentley, No 31639 waits for the 'S15' to attach to the train, after which it will follow light to Alton. *Les Price*

No 31639 brought us back tender first, arriving at Bentley five minutes early, which allowed plenty of time for the change of locomotives with No 30837 coming back to the front. No 31639 did not for the present join us as it was due to follow 'light' to Alton. Even allowing for the five minutes in hand we were a minute late, departing at 11.53am for the short run to Alton.

At Alton there was a scheduled 24-minute wait, to allow No 31639 to arrive and then manoeuvre inside next to the coaches, the 'S15' still the leading engine. We left three minutes late, doubtless due to having to shepherd eager participants back on board.

Left: **Ready for departure south from Alton towards the fearsome 1 in 60 climb to Medstead.** *Les Price*

Opposite page: **Coming and going on Medstead bank. No 30837 leads No 31639 on the climb with eight vehicles in tow, with some recording the sound.** *Roger Thornton*

'USA' No 30073 coming on to the special to take it into the works sidings. This engine had been used for the same purpose on the previous Sunday. *Les Price*

Compared with the previous week, 14 minutes had been allowed for the four-and-a-half-mile climb of 200 feet up to Medstead Home Signal, two more minutes than the previous week. But with the extra power the pair stormed the bank in 12 minutes. At Medstead we crossed the scheduled 11.53am Southampton-Alton, a two-car 'Hampshire' DEMU.

We arrived at Eastleigh and 'USA' 0-6-0T No 30073 took us into the Loco Works Yard where we were free to roam for the next hour and a half; conveniently a number of mini staircases complete with handrails had been provided to facilitate passengers descending from the coaches.

My brother and I stuck to the Depot, taking a number of photographs. Among these was 'M7' No 30053. I had previously seen this engine in July 1964, when I happened to photograph her running through Kempton Park as she travelled to Shepperton at the head of the LCGB 'Surrey Rambler Railtour', at the time in much better fettle than when we saw her in 1966. However, she was destined for preservation.

Right: **'M7' No 30053, which together with 'Schools' No 30926 was at the time stored at Eastleigh pending preservation in Canada.** *Les Price*

Opposite: **A pause at Alresford in the sunshine; unfortunately it would not last.** *Roger Thornton*

Another image taken was of a youthful fireman on No 31639 emptying out its smokebox close to the Eastleigh coaling road. Coincidentally some 22 years later, I met a new colleague at work; his name was Mick Foster and it soon became apparent we shared the same interest in railways. One day I happened to show that particular Eastleigh photograph to Mick who immediately said, 'That's me'. Our friendship was forged, consequently I contacted him asking for his own recollections of the day.

'At the time I was living at home in Farnham. I was just 17 years of age and had awoken that morning to find a covering of snow on the ground. I knew I had to be at Guildford by 8.30am; the roster had been published on the previous Friday, and I knew I was for a special duty.

'I lived about a mile from Farnham station so cycled along the straight and down the hill over snow sprinkled roads to the station and caught an "Up" train to Woking about 6am. This was probably the first "Up" train of the day on a Sunday which would have arrived at Woking at about 6.30am.

'On arrival I learnt that, for whatever reason, no trains were running on the mainline down to Guildford, probably because of the overnight snow. Concerned I telephoned the signalman who told me that nothing was booked, not even a light engine. On reflection, knowing that I was working a "special", I probably rang the loco depot to let them know I was on my way.

'Knowing that I was going to work a "Special" obviously motivated me so there was nothing for it but to walk the six miles along the line to Guildford. I guess this would have taken me about 90 minutes; a mixture of jogging and brisk walking; not easy on a railway formation.

'Nothing came by until I was walking down Stoughton bank approaching Guildford station when a "Q" class, running tender first and light engine, came trundling past. It had its storm sheet up providing some protection to the crew from the icy breeze, the result of which was probably why the crew failed to see me. Even so I still managed to arrive at the shed on time for my turn, not knowing what it actually was until I

Mick Foster shovelling ashes out of the smokebox of No 31639 in front of the office block at Eastleigh. *Les Price*

booked on. It was only then I learnt it was the LCGB Special Train. My Driver was Sid Woods.

'Our engine was No 31639, one of the last remaining "U" class locomotives; fortunately it had already been prepared and was awaiting us on shed. I sorted out the fire, checked the water level in the tender and trimmed the coal. We then took water and another skip of coal. For the run to Bentley we went via Ash, Aldershot and Farnham and on arrival waited for the special from London. I remember vividly our run through the rural Surrey and Hampshire countryside enveloped in that canopy of snow.

'At Bentley we stood at the "Up" platform, while the "S15" ran in on the "Down" line. What I did notice was that almost the moment the train stopped there were rail enthusiasts all over the place. We took the train on down to Bordon, ran round, and then tender first back to Bentley. At Bordon, and back at Bentley, the scenes were repeated, people everywhere straddling the running rails, "Up" and "Down" roads, even the juice rails; it was amazing nobody was electrocuted.

'I distinctly remember having a good start from Alton with the "S15" in front and storming up Medstead bank. Speeding through Winchester with our engine driven from the right-hand side, I had time to lean out of the cab and see the joy on the faces of passengers on the platform as two old Southern Railway locomotives flew through the station with whistles blasting.

'All too soon we arrived at Eastleigh and a "USA" tank took the train into the works. We went on to the shed where Sid and I disposed of our locomotive, checking the oil points, cleaning the fire, the smoke box and ash pan. After bidding farewell to our engine we travelled back to Guildford "on the cushions" with a certain sense of satisfaction at a job well done!'

Back on the tour once the 'USA' had taken my brother and I back to the station, the 'S15' again took up its position at the head of the train. We left Eastleigh four minutes late and headed 'Down' the original LSWR line towards Gosport. From Fareham we headed for Cosham Junction where we forked left over the spur to Farlington Junction. We had passed Cosham five minutes late, but by Havant were only three minutes down.

The winter evening was now closing in. We began to run early through to Guildford, where we stopped to take on water. Six minutes had been allowed for this, but most of the enthusiasts stuck to the cosy warmth of their seats rather than venturing out into the darkness of a winter's night.

From Guildford we ran steadily on to Waterloo arriving on time at 5.40pm. By now Mick Foster was back at home enjoying his Sunday dinner and those on the train were reflecting on their last trip behind an 'S15' and indeed, one of the last ever runs behind a pair of ex-Southern Railway locomotives.

Despite acquitting themselves well on this tour both the 'S15' and the 'U' failed to make it into preservation. The 'S15' had already been previously withdrawn but had been retained for special workings and, despite her good external appearance, others of the class had already been preferred. The 'U' was withdrawn less than six months after the tour and also met the cutter's torch.

Crewkerne's Calf Float

Jeffery Grayer

Jeffery Grayer **recalls this quaint piece of BR kit used to assist in ferrying calves from farm lorry to railway train.**

Cattle traffic had for long been a staple of BR's freight operations with special wagons being constructed for their transport. A little known and little photographed aspect of these workings was the operation of 'Calf Floats' which were used to move calves and other small livestock from the road transport, which had brought the beasts from the farm into the station yard, on to the cattle dock which, in the case of Crewkerne, was situated on the down side of the station yard, and so ready for loading into a horsebox or cattle wagon.

Calf floats had their origin in the days when BR were 'common carriers' obliged to transport virtually any goods offered to them. On the former LSWR mainline from Salisbury to Exeter livestock was an important traffic for many years and most stations forwarded live cattle, sheep and pigs to market with Exeter, Salisbury, Yeovil and Gillingham being particularly important local destinations. That at Gillingham was particularly renowned for being one of the largest calf markets in the country. After market much of the sold stock was herded back to the local station for onward transmission to abattoirs, one of these being at Maiden Lane on the North London line.

With Crewkerne station situated about one mile from the town centre, cattle could be herded up the main road to the down side yard at the station where cattle trucks would be waiting to transport them more often than not to London. Calves were the particular speciality of one local Beaminster farmer, Sam Gibbs, who regularly forwarded these youngsters by rail from Crewkerne, their destination generally being Maud in Scotland. Horseboxes were positioned adjacent to the cattle dock usually by the locomotive of the 2.40pm Yeovil Junction-Chard Junction freight service. After loading they were then moved on to the down mainline from where the locomotive of the 3.25pm passenger service from Exeter to Templecombe collected them, having reversed over the crossover from the up line. (This explains why a horsebox was used, as these vehicles were vacuum-fitted and so could be used as 'tail traffic'.)

This example of a calf float was captured at Crewkerne station during the 1950s. Note the central pair of wheels with a single wheel at the front and small supporting wheel at the rear, the rudimentary springing and the brake mechanism with the wooden brake block. It was lettered 'CALF FLOAT B.R. s Crewkerne'.

Calf float exhibit, with stock on board and marked
'Portsmouth Harbour – Ryde Pierhead only', on the IoWSR
at Havenstreet. *Jacqueline Banerjee – Victorian web*

At Templecombe they were sent northwards over the S&D route and the Midland line on their long journey to Scotland. Maud boasted the largest one-day fat-stock market in the whole of the UK and every Wednesday more than 1,000 cattle and up to 5,000 sheep were sold as farmers from across Scotland flocked to the small Aberdeenshire village. However, changes in the supply chain, outbreaks of BSE and Foot and Mouth disease finally put paid to the Maud market, which closed in 2001. In recent years there has been increasing emphasis on fattening and slaughtering animals as close to their home locality as possible and groups such as Compassion in World Farming are seeking to promote the message that transporting live animals vast distances is inhumane.

The switch to shipping fresh killed meat as early as the 1930s caused a steady reduction in live cattle traffic and in 1962 British Railways reduced the number of stations open for livestock from over two and a half thousand nationally to just over two hundred. By the late 1960s only live cattle imported from Ireland were still being moved by rail and this too came to an end when that trade ceased in 1975. To have fresh meat in days gone by, an animal had to be slaughtered and butchered in close proximity to where it was going to be processed and sold. With improvements in refrigeration, packaging and transportation it became more economical for meat processors to handle livestock at a limited number of processing factories and to ship the finished product to market, rather than having to handle meat 'on the hoof'.

Cattle were sometimes moved as block loads right up to the end of the railway's involvement in this traffic but most cattle wagons travelled in small numbers either attached to goods trains or occasionally to passenger trains on branch lines where mixed working was permitted. They would generally be found grouped together at the locomotive end of any consist as this meant they could easily be shunted directly to the cattle dock on arrival where the animals could then be fed and watered.

[Ed: I'm amazed that a Dorset farmer would have sent livestock to market at Maud, of all places – it's all but a 'Land's End to John o' Groats' journey: and no matter how carefully the animals were fed and watered during the journey (and very little else could have been done), they must have lost condition and value on so long a trip.]

An example of a calf float has been preserved on the Isle of Wight Steam Railway. This particular float originated from Salisbury before subsequent transfer to Portsmouth Harbour station, where it was used to transfer animals from train to the Isle of Wight ferry. Repainted in the mid-1960s into the new corporate blue livery, it was modified by the addition of lifting eyes at each corner to enable it to be craned aboard the ferries. However, after a couple of years livestock traffic was transferred to the car ferry service to Fishbourne and it became redundant. It then found a new lease of life acting as a suitable carrying device for tools and timber required by the Portsmouth Harbour pier maintenance gang. It subsequently passed to the IoWSR where it was stored for a number of years but is now on display at the Train Story Visitor Centre at Havenstreet station. A life-size model calf on loan from the Cow Company collection at Tapnell Farm Park near Yarmouth (IoW) has been placed in the float to aid interpretation of the exhibit. It is believed that this calf float is one of very few still in existence and as such is an important historical artefact.

Book Review

Gilbert Szlumper and Leo Amery of the Southern Railway

John King, Published by Pen & Sword, 2018. £25.00
ISBN 978 1473835276. 221 sides, casebound

I will admit I had a number of pre-conceived notions upon being sent this book for review. Initially the question was, would it have been a book I would likely have bought 'on-spec'? The answer was probably 'no' but it also goes to show how wrong an assessment can be – made, I will admit, with no prior knowledge.

So where to start? Well, if you are looking for a book full of new railway pictures from the period you will be disappointed. This is not a pictorial work; in fact I might even venture to say the images (well reproduced though they are) add little to the structure of the work.

But to the principal positive points, here is a book about a man, Szlumper, 'in the know', and in a position similar to that of Walker and later Elliott, a senior figure within Southern Railway management and whose diaries reveal far more than might comfortably have been said at the time.

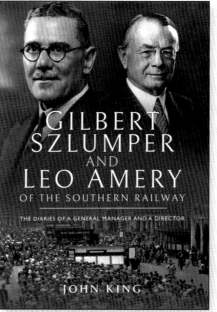

We may think of the Southern Railway as being clean, swish and efficient in the late 1930s but the reality was in fact somewhat different. We learn for example the trains and stations were dirty and unkempt, of the bullying behaviour of Ellson the CCE to his subordinates, of Billinton's attempt to cajole favour after the retirement of Maunsell and offer himself as CME, and the often strained relations between senior officers who really should have known better.

An embittered man might be expected to make such comments but we should recall these are contemporary to the period and precede the time when Szlumper had left the Southern. There is also detail of his unsuccessful attempt to return a few years later – a time when Missenden, as Szlumper's successor as General Manager, had negotiated a clause in his own contract to the effect that he could not be demoted or moved to a lowlier post.

As regards Amery and the memoirs reported, here was an ambitious man who perhaps regarded himself as possessing greater ability than he actually had. The inclusion of his time as a Director arguably adds balance to the book but in reality there is little of real substance. It is the Szlumper notes alone that are worth their weight in gold.

We also have a most interesting insight into the behaviour of railway managers from other companies in World War 2, individuals – and yes names are often mentioned – who even in the dark days of the war were at times unwilling, or unable, to focus fully on the needs of the day. Szlumper, for example, has some scathing comments to make about a senior officer from the LNER who seemed to have a preoccupation with the size of toilets in new rolling stock, whilst the man from the GWR was described as (having) 'too much drink and not enough energy'.

There are numerous such quips which come together to form an interesting viewpoint. It would be very tempting to add more examples but that would be unfair to the author and publisher. Instead, if you want something genuinely different, this is well worth a read.